WORLD WAR II
IN COLOR

From the Eastern Front to the Pacific—The War in 300 Color Photographs

WORLD WAR II
IN COLOR

From the Eastern Front to the Pacific—The War in 300 Color Photographs

Gina McNeely   Jon Guttman

Elephant Book
Company

© 2010 by Elephant Book Company Limited

This edition published by Elephant Book Company Limited,
35 Fournier Street, London, E1 6QE, United Kingdom.

Editorial Director: Will Steeds
Project Editor: Chris Stone
Designer: Philip Clucas
Copy Editor: Karen Stein
Additional picture research: Susannah Jayes
Production: Robert Paulley
Proofreader: Julia North

Color reproduction: Modern Age Repro House Ltd,
Hong Kong

Elephant Book Company Limited,
35 Fournier Street,
London, E1 6QE,
United Kingdom

ISBN: 978-0-9552720-1-1

Printed and bound in China

10 9 8 7 6 5 4 3 2 1

Contents

Introduction

Until the invention of the camera in 1839, the depiction of warfare was literally an art, subject to the agenda of the artist or his sponsors. The earliest-known photographs of conflict were1846 daguerreotypes of soldiers during the Mexican-American War, British troops in Burma and India in 1848–52, Russians during their invasion of Ottoman-held Romanian territory in 1853–45, and battlefield views of the Crimean War in 1855.

It was during the American Civil War of 1861–65 that photographers such as Mathew Brady, Alexander Gardner, and Timothy O'Sullivan began to subject the public to warfare's grislier side as they ventured toward the battle lines, although even then the lens was only as objective as the eye that selected its subjects. For a poignant shot of a Confederate sharpshooter slain in the Devil's Den at Gettysburg, for example, Gardner or one of his team dragged the subject some 35 yards (32m) to the desired location—an act that would now be regarded as a violation of honest photojournalism in the strictest sense.

As the state of the art of black and white photography advanced, it became an indispensable tool to armies for gathering intelligence as well as for the photographers, military and civilian, who recorded their operations. By World War II, film had completely replaced the glass plate negative; film, lenses, and shutter speeds were faster; cameras were lighter, less bulky, and no longer dependent on tripods. All this gave the skilled photographer greater mobility and flexibility for capturing the moments that turned up and vanished with equal suddenness in the fast-moving environment of 20th-century mechanized warfare. Another dramatic innovation in 1943 was the introduction of radio photo, a telephoto electronic transmission service that made it possible to transmit images across the Atlantic Ocean in about seven minutes.

Above: Hugo Jaeger, seen here in 1970, was Adolf Hitler's personal photographer, taking some 2,000 color photos of the *Führer*, as well as propaganda shots of the *Wehrmacht* in action. After the fall of the Third Reich in May 1945, he stashed his photographs in a leather suitcase and, after slipping past American soldiers—who were more interested in the bottle of cognac they found than in the bag's other contents—he sealed the photos in 12 jars and buried them outside Munich until 1955, when he dug them up. Jaeger sold the photos to *LIFE* magazine 10 years later, but they were not published until June 2009, around the 65th anniversary of the D-Day landings in Normandy.

Below: A US Navy chief photographer's mate instructs a student on using a hand-held camera before a North American SNJ-4 trainer at the Naval School of Photography at Naval Air Station Pensacola, Florida, in February 1944. More than 5,000 photographers served in the Navy, at training stations, on bases, and in Combat Photographic Units (CPUs) overseas, attached to warships and aviation units.

Back during World War I, a major innovation arose in the form of color photography, although the process at that time was time consuming and expensive, resulting in few color photos being made. That state of the art, too, had advanced by World War II, but even then the amount of color photographs represents a small fraction of the millions taken in the course of the conflict. Most were motion pictures, but a lot of Kodachrome-type transparencies were taken by the Germans, the British, United States Army and Navy photographers, and, to a lesser extent, the Italians. Few other photographers used color in combat, however. Its greater expense aside, color film took longer to develop, was vulnerable to heat and other atmospheric conditions, was relatively hard to ship to the front, and ran an equally daunting gauntlet home for development at facilities such as the Rochester Institute of Technology in New York.

In view of this, a history of World War II told in color represents the culmination of a protracted, often hazardous,

Above: Staff Sergeant Brush poses with a K-20 camera in the waist gunner's position of a Boeing B-17. Aerial cameramen had challenge enough keeping their tools steady in a moving airplane, let alone a bomber bucked by flak bursts or under attack by enemy fighters. The fruits of their labors, however, were militarily useful for mission assessment, staff reports, and training, as well as propaganda. In 1944, Lieutenant Colonel William Wyler's filming of the 25th mission of the Eighth Air Force B-17F *Memphis Belle* became one of the classic documentaries of all time.

and sometimes fatal process by which thousands of dedicated, courageous, professional cameramen captured a variety of wartime facets on film. Among them was the author's father, Photographer's Mate Third Class Paul D. Guttman, a US Navy combat photographer on detached duty from the 59th Construction Battalion who worked under one of the great lensmen of both world wars—and a personal idol of Guttman's long before Pearl Harbor—Edward Steichen. Taking on a variety of assignments on land, on sea, in the air, and, for several weeks, *under* the sea aboard the submarine *Spot*, Paul Guttman

continuously carried his camera into harm's way from Kwajalein in January 1944 through Okinawa in June 1945. Many of his black-and-white shots were memorable; alas, the bulk of his color was of the motion picture variety, some of which, taken aboard the aircraft carrier *Yorktown*, was used in Steichen's Academy Award-winning wartime documentary film *The Fighting Lady*.

Perhaps typically, Dad confessed to being as scared as any normal serviceman would have been throughout the fighting, but, as was the case with the average soldier, sailor, or airman, the mission, the job, overcame his fear. "When I was taking pictures," he used to say, "the battlefield seemed to be limited to what I saw through the camera lens." Still, there were occasions when reality interfered with his work. On Kwajalein, he had to kill a Japanese officer who only failed to shoot him because his Nambu Type 98 pistol had misfired (Dad kept the pistol). While occupying the gunner's seat in various aircraft he shot down at least three enemy planes. At Saipan on July 16, 1944, he put his camera aside to rush out onto the beach and carry two wounded Marines out of the line of fire. His reaction to receiving the Silver Star for that act some 55 years later—and being reminded of the reason by my reading the accompanying citation to him twice—elicited a reaction typical of his comrades-in-arms: "Oh, that! What'd they give me a medal for that for? Everybody was doing that! You see a couple of your guys cut down . . . what else do you do?"

Such is just one of the stories behind the photographs that make up this volume. At the same time, however, it must be confessed up front that it is impossible to present a comprehensive treatment of the war's events by the exclusive use of color, because such a collection of photographs would not be comprehensive. Soviet combat cameramen, for example, did not use color film at all, so a color treatment of their front is dominated by the Germans, whose work had to be cleared through Dr. Josef Goebbels's propaganda ministry and consequently tended to put the best possible face on things, even as the German forces were being pushed inexorably westward toward Berlin. A similar imbalance exists between the plethora of American color footage of the war in the Pacific and the near nonexistence of images from the Japanese viewpoint.

Whenever possible, the author has tried to restore some perspective in the brief stories behind the pictures. Even then, the effectiveness of such verbal attempts may inevitably pale beside the emotive impact of the images themselves.

Above: Corporal Marshall Hull of the 196th Signal Photo Company takes a knee beside 16-inch (400mm) shells used by the coastal defense guns at the Tuscan port of Viareggio. The US Army Signal Corps started out with four photo companies in 1942 but soon had to create more. It also purchased the old Paramount film studio in Astoria, Long Island, New York, to process incoming photos. By the end of the war the Signal Corps, whose ranks included Hollywood directors Colonel Darryl Zanuck, Major Frank Capra, and Lieutenant John Huston, had produced 1,338 films as well as 500,000 still photographs.

Chapter 1

The Road to War

In some respects, World War II was both a continuation and a consequence of World War I. Japan and Italy, both Allied powers, sought to expand their wartime gains. Germans resented the punishing restrictions imposed on them by the 1919 Treaty of Versailles. Exacerbating the situation was the ideological struggle that attended the rise of international Communism and, in reaction, the equally despotic but more nationally oriented fascist movement, starting with Benito Mussolini's rise to power in Italy between 1922 and 1925, followed by Adolf Hitler's in Germany in 1933.

The League of Nations, established after World War I, proved impotent in the face of aggressive acts such as Japan's invasion of Manchuria in 1931–32; Germany's resumption of rearmament in 1935; Italy's conquest of Ethiopia in 1935–36; Soviet, Italian, and German intervention in the Spanish Civil War from 1936 to 1939; Japan's invasion of China in 1937; and Germany's forceful Anschluss ("union") with Austria in 1938.

After promising no further territorial demands to British Prime Minister Neville Chamberlain and French President Edouard Daladier, Hitler occupied the Czechoslovakian Sudetenland in October 1938—and went on to occupy and dismember Czechoslovakia in March 1939. Hungary also seized territory from eastern Slovakia in March 1939, and Italy overran Albania in April.

A much-overlooked conflict of future import began when a border clash between Soviet ally Mongolia and Japanese-dominated Manchuria flared into undeclared war in August, ending in ceasefire on September 15 with the Japanese army defeated by a rare survivor of Josef Stalin's military purges, Lieutenant General Georgy Zhukov. As a result of this setback, the Japanese abandoned its army's "Northern Strategy" against the Soviet Union in favor of the navy-advocated "Southern Strategy" to seize the Asian and Pacific holdings of Britain, France, the Netherlands, and the United States.

Right: In St. Johns, Arizona, surplus food is distributed to Americans long out of work amid the Great Depression, whose global economic effects influenced the rise of communist, socialist, and fascist governments throughout Europe. Poverty played into the hands of extremist elements who blended it in with other forms of popular discontent within their respective countries, such as the runaway inflation that befell Germany's Weimar Republic in the 1920s, or the widespread Italian belief that it had not achieved all the territorial gains it deserved for its participation in World War I.

Right: The succession of "New Deal" programs launched by President Franklin Delano Roosevelt—shown at his desk in Albany while still governor of New York in 1932—were not always effective, but they generally raised public morale and averted the rise of more radical movements within the United States. Among the agencies he created, the Farm Security Administration, combined with the Federal Writers' Project, documented progress throughout the American heartland, taking 164,000 photographs, of which 1,600 were in color. When war broke out, in 1942 the FSA and FWP were incorporated into the Office of War Information.

Opposite page: Thousands of cheering participants greet the *Führer* at one of the great rallies held in Nuremberg in 1938. As Hitler's nationalistically and racially motivated programs mobilized the populace toward effecting German economic recovery, success bred success. Paralleling the economic recovery, however, was an equally ambitious rearmament program—at first furtive, but later openly defiant of the Versailles Treaty, after 1935. The ultimate goal of Hitler and his followers was the fulfillment of the Teutonic Aryan's destiny as the "Master Race."

Left: Benito Mussolini (left) is shown here visiting Adolf Hitler in Munich in 1938. The Italian dictator selectively combined capitalism with government-controlled socialism. His goal was to establish a fascist government in Italy through his election as prime minister in 1922, and his gradual seizure of absolute power by 1925. His fostering of an aggressive Italian nationalism—aimed at reviving the Roman Empire and control of the Mediterranean under the ancient Roman slogan of *"Mare Nostrum"* (Our Sea) inspired Hitler to set Germany on a similar path in central and eastern Europe.

Left: A Jewish business on Berlin's Potsdamer Strasse lies demolished on November 10, 1938, in the wake of the anti-Semitic riots that came to be called *Kristallnacht* ("crystal night") for the broken glass that littered the streets. The Nazi use of Jews as scapegoats for Germany's troubles soon evolved into a systematic program aimed at their complete extermination worldwide, the realization of which would be zealously pursued by Hitler's chief of the SS, or *Schutz Staffel* ("protection squadron," in essence an Aryan Nazi Praetorian Guard), *Reichsführer* Heinrich Himmler.

Right: A German glider enthusiast undergoes the clandestine beginning of training that will ultimately qualify him as a pilot in the Nazi *Luftwaffe*. After denouncing the Versailles Treaty's disarmament clause in a speech to the Reichstag on May 17, 1933, Hitler openly violated it in the spring of 1935 with a massive rearmament program. The *Luftwaffe* underwent a dramatic transformation into a modern, powerful military arm with such advanced warplanes as the Messerschmitt Bf-109B fighter and Dornier Do-17E bomber. German armored fighting vehicles and the doctrine for their employment also progressed, while the German navy's ships, though modest in number, impressed foreign observers with their construction, armament, and efficiency.

Opposite page: Hugo Jaeger took this photograph of British Prime Minister Neville Chamberlain's arrival in Munich on September 28, 1938, to meet with Hitler over the latter's threats to seize the ethnically German Sudetenland from Czechoslovakia. Portrayed from the left are *Gauleiter* ("Party Leader") Adolf Wagner, *Sturmabteilung-Obergruppenführer* ("Stormtrooper Senior Leader") Franz Ritter von Epp, German Foreign Minister Joachim von Ribbentropp, Chamberlain, and British Ambassador Sir Neville Henderson. At 1:30 a.m. on September 30, Chamberlain, Hitler, Mussolini, and French President Edouard Daladier signed an agreement assenting to the takeover, which was popularly hailed at the time (except in Czechoslovakia, which had had no say in the matter) for having assuaged German ambitions and averted war.

Left: Veterans of the Condor Legion—Germans sent to fight alongside an Italian contingent in support of Spanish Nationalists led by General Francisco Franco Bahomonde after their revolt against the leftist Republican government on July 17, 1936—return bearing plaques with the names of comrades killed in action following the fall of the Republic on April 1, 1939. Aside from the ideological struggle it entailed, the Spanish Civil War was used by the Germans and Italians—as well as Soviet servicemen aiding the Republicans—to test their latest weaponry, hone their tactical and strategic doctrine, and gain combat experience.

Above: After choosing to open up to the West in 1871, Japan set itself on a course of eclipsing the Western powers in East Asia, one by one, starting with Russia in 1905 and Germany in 1914. Emperor Hirohito, shown in 1947, encouraged a renewed militarism. This led to the invasion of Manchuria on September 19, 1931, whose condemnation by the League of Nations was ignored by the Japanese; Japan established a puppet regime in what they renamed Manchukuo in 1932 and left the League in March 1933. In July 1937 the Japanese invaded China, where their atrocities against civilians shocked the outside world and set them on a collision course with the Western powers, particularly the United States.

Left: German troops enter a Sudeten village in October 1938, following the Munich agreements. Far from being satisfied with the Sudentenland, on March 15, 1939, Hitler occupied all of Czechoslovakia, annexing Bohemia and Moravia as German "protectorates" while allowing Slovakia to exist as a separate, pro-German republic. On March 23, Slovakia got a taste of its own medicine when Hungary invaded its eastern territories, precipitating a brief war that ended with a ceasefire on March 31 and a German-brokered peace between its two potential allies on April 4, in which Slovakia ceded away 1,054 square miles (1,697 sq km) and 69,930 purportedly Hungarian inhabitants.

Right: A sergeant stands by his gun as part of the US Coastal Defenses. After Secretary of State Henry Stimson's refusal to recognize Japan's puppet state of Manchukuo on January 7, 1932, the bulk of spending on coastal installations centered on the West Coast from 1933 to 1938, including 400mm guns with 25-mile (40km) range under thick concrete casemates and vegetation for camouflage. The rising German threat led to bolstering established fortifications on the East Coast. When war broke out, however, the greatest threat off the United States' shores would be submarines, against which the big guns were virtually useless.

Below: Marine recruits complete training at Parris Island, South Carolina, in May 1942. Fighting alongside the US Army's Second Infantry Division during World War I gave the Marines their first experience against comparably equipped and trained opponents, adding Belleau Wood to their laurels. Their participation in minor Central American "Banana Wars" during the 1920s gave the Marines some exposure to jungle warfare against elusive guerrillas, but it proved to be scant preparation for the ordeal they would soon undergo in the Pacific.

Opposite page: Resisting a strong isolationist movement, President Roosevelt reinitiated American preparations for what he regarded as inevitable involvement in a coming war with Germany or Japan. This began in earnest on September 14, 1940, when Congress passed the country's first peacetime draft, requiring all males between ages 21 and 30 to register for military service, enlistment to be determined by lottery. After the United States entered the war in December 1941, the age limits were extended to 18 at the youngest and 45 at the oldest. The 1918-vintage helmets and spurs on members of this horse-drawn 75mm pack howitzer crew engaged in a prewar training exercise suggest how much catching up the US Army needed to do.

Right: A crew trainee mans a machine-gun position aboard a preproduction Boeing YB-17. When the prototype Model 299 first flew on July 28, 1935, Richard Williams of the *Seattle Times* dubbed it a "Flying Fortress," a sobriquet Boeing quickly copyrighted for its innovative four-engine bomber. The 13 YB-17s ordered on January 17, 1936, featured a speed of 256mph (411kph), a 30,600-foot (9,326m) ceiling, and a 3,320-mile (5,343km) range, along with five .30-caliber machine guns. The 155 B-17s of various models produced by November 30, 1941, was only the beginning—by May 1945 that total would rise to 12,731.

Left: Student pilots draw parachutes for a training flight at Naval Air Station Pensacola, Florida. The coming war would see these airmen evolve from an adjunct to the vital punch of the US Navy. At the end of 1941, the first American aircraft carrier, *Langley*, had been converted into a seaplane tender, and the rest of the carrier fleet consisted of *Lexington, Saratoga, Ranger, Yorktown, Enterprise, Wasp,* and *Hornet*. Of them, only *Ranger* and *Wasp* would see action outside of the Pacific theater of operations.

Right: The newly launched submarine *Swordfish* (SS193) slips down the ways at Mare Island, California, on April 3, 1939. The US Navy had 50 submarines in the Pacific when Pearl Harbor plunged it into the war, and nine days later, on December 16, 1941, *Swordfish* was the first to sink a Japanese vessel, cargo ship *Atsutasan Maru*. It went on to sink or damage 27 others, including the destroyer *Matsukaze*, before disappearing with all hands during its 13th war patrol in January 1945.

Chapter 2

Worldwide Conflagration

Opposite page: In reaction to American trade sanctions against shipments of strategic resources to aid Japan's invasion of China, the Japanese militarists embarked on an audacious offensive to drive all Western powers from Asia and the Pacific and seize their assets for themselves. Their first move was a carrier-launched surprise attack on the US fleet at Pearl Harbor, Hawaii, on December 7, 1941. The eight battleships that were sunk or damaged included the USS *West Virginia* (foreground) and *Tennessee*, but only the USS *Arizona* and *Oklahoma* were permanently lost.

Poland strongly opposed Hitler's invasion on September 1, 1939, and France and Britain promptly declared war. Still, Germany's new *Blitzkrieg* strategy overwhelmed Poland's forces; in addition, the Soviet Union invaded the country on September 17.

Using his nonaggression pact with Hitler to prepare for the showdown both knew had merely been postponed, Stalin incorporated Bessarabia, Estonia, Latvia, and Lithuania into the Soviet Union, but his army, upon invading Finland on November 30, 1939, suffered galling defeats before the Finns capitulated on March 13, 1940. Hitler saw the Russo-Finnish Winter War as proof of the Red Army's ineptitude—and the need to take advantage of it without delay. First, however, he had to deal with the West.

On April 9, the Germans invaded Denmark and Norway; on May 10 they invaded Belgium, the Netherlands, and France, the latter surrendering on June 23. Now alone, Britain managed to fend off the German onslaught between July and October 1940, in a campaign waged primarily in the air.

Italy entered the war on June 10, 1940, but in short order its forces in North Africa were routed, its October 28 invasion of Greece thrown back, its battle fleet torpedoed in Taranto Harbor by British carrier planes on November 11, and its African colonies of Ethiopia and Somaliland lost by May 1941. Hitler sent Erwin Rommel to aid his ally in North Africa, and between April and late May 1941, the *Wehrmacht* overran Yugoslavia, Greece, and Crete—the latter featuring in history's first airborne conquest of an island.

On June 22, 1941, Hitler launched Operation Barbarossa, a massive invasion of Russia that almost reached Moscow before being driven back on December 6. The next morning, a surprise attack by Japanese carrier planes on the naval base at Pearl Harbor drew the United States into the conflict.

Left: Soon after the German invasion of Poland on September 1, 1939, Polish soldiers swept up in the onslaught gather in a prisoner holding compound. Contrary to myths of cavalry charging tanks, Poland entered the war with its own arsenal of modern weapons, including the PZL P-37 medium bomber and the 7TP tank. What the Polish forces lacked were the communications and coordination to match the *Blitzkrieg* ("lightning war") strategy employed by the Germans—a well-orchestrated combined-arms mechanized onslaught calculated to give the enemy no time to rest or regroup.

Bottom left: German infantry prepare for another advance outside Warsaw on September 17, 1939. On that same day, in accordance with its "Non-Aggression Pact" signed with the Germans on August 23, the Soviet Union invaded Poland from the other side. Slovakia had also contributed some 50,000 troops on the invasion's first day. The Germans suffered 16,343 dead in the fighting, compared to 66,000 Polish military personnel and between 150,000 and 200,000 civilians, some 20,000 of whom were murdered by special units, or *Einsatztruppen*. Of those captured by the Soviets, at least 22,436 Polish military officers, intellectuals, policemen, and public officials were secretly murdered by the NKVD at Katyn and other locations.

Opposite page (top): *Panzerkampfwagen* ("armored battle vehicle"—or tank) Mark Is parade through the partially bombed-out city of Warsaw on October 5, 1939. The Polish government never formally surrendered and, while the Germans began an exceedingly brutal occupation of their country, thousands of Poles escaped to carry on the fight in France, Britain and—after the Germans invaded it on June 22, 1941—the Soviet Union. Others would form guerrilla units, including the *Armija Krajowa*, or Home Army, the largest domestic resistance force in Europe.

Left: *Gebirgsjäger*, or mountain troops, patrol the Norwegian mountains as the Germans consolidate their hold on that country. Requiring a combined effort by the army, navy and *Luftwaffe*, the German invasions of Denmark and Norway were completed between April and June 1940, in the face of British and French as well as Norwegian opposition. The German *Kriegsmarine*, or navy, suffered the galling losses of the heavy cruiser *Blücher,* light cruisers *Karlsrühe* and *Königsberg*, and ten destroyers during the campaign, but during the Allied evacuation on June 8, the British aircraft carrier *Glorious* and its destroyer escorts, *Acasta* and *Ardent*, were caught and sunk by battle cruisers *Scharnhorst* and *Gneisenau.*

Right: British soldiers stationed in Iceland undergo mortar practice. Although an autonomous Danish possession, Iceland declared neutrality after Denmark fell, but the British, fearing that it would come under German occupation, landed 746 Royal Marines on the island on May 10, 1940. British forces in Iceland eventually rose to 25,000 until July 7, 1941, when the still-neutral United States replaced them with 40,000 of its own troops, securing it against possible use by the Germans, who might otherwise seize it to aid their U-boat operations in the North Atlantic.

Opposite page (center): Firemen battle the flames in a Royal Dutch Shell oil reservoir after a German bombing attack on Amsterdam. On May 10, the same day Winston Churchill became Britain's new Prime Minister, the Germans invaded the Netherlands. Although the Dutch put up a spirited fight, the last of their forces had laid down their arms by May 17. Neighboring Belgium was overrun in two weeks. Both of their governments went into exile, joining the Poles in England. That left the Netherlands government still in possession of the East Indies, including the Sumatran oil fields of Palembang and Balikpapan.

Above: Patrolling Icelandic waters in the summer of 1941, the crew of a 3-inch/50 caliber antiaircraft gun aboard the US Navy battleship *New York* keeps an eye out for four-engine German Focke Wulf Fw-200C Condors, which guided U-boats to Allied convoys or bombed the shipping themselves. Though still nominally neutral, Reykjavik often provided an interim airbase for Allied aircraft crossing the Atlantic. On June 17, 1944, Iceland severed ties with occupied Denmark entirely and declared itself an independent republic.

Right: The inner city of Rotterdam lies in ruins after being struck by 1,308 bombs dropped by 54 Heinkel He-111Hs of *Kampfgeschwader* (battle wing) 54 on May 14, 1940. The attack killed 813 civilians, destroyed 24,000 houses, and left 80,000 residents homeless. Hitler had ordered the strike that morning in response to the city's stubborn resistance, but later in the day the Dutch had offered to negotiate surrender terms with the German Sixth Army, which tried to stop the attack with radio and flares. Sadly, only 36 aircraft got the message and aborted. Consequently, on the night of May 15 the Royal Air Force, which hitherto had only bombed targets of direct military importance, attacked industrial cities in the German Ruhr Valley. A precedent had been set for bombing civilian targets for the rest of the war.

Right: The Germans unearth strongpoints along the vaunted Maginot Line after their conquest of France. For months after the invasion of Poland, German troops faced the French and steadily arriving British Expeditionary Force across France's eastern frontier in a generally passive standoff that the French called *"Le Drôle de Guerre,"* the Germans called the *"Sitzkrieg,"* and the British named the "Phony War." When the Germans finally made their move, their highly mobile force did not directly assault the Maginot Line's reputedly impregnable network of fortified underground defenses but simply went around them.

Above: Refugees flee the fighting as the German invaders overrun Belgium, the Netherlands, and northern France, with Junkers Ju-87B Stukas often attacking them to add to the general panic. In a reprise of General Alfred von Schlieffen's plan from World War I, Hitler's *Wehrmacht* again tried to circumvent France's eastern defenses with an end run from the north. This time, however, as British and French forces massed to meet the northern threat, a different German force was entering France from another, unexpected direction.

Above right: The crew of a Panzer IV medium tank takes a brief rest in the Ardennes during the lightning thrust through that seemingly impassible forest. Devised by *Generalleutnant* Erich von Manstein, refined by *Generalleutnant* Heinz Guderian, and approved by Hitler over the objections of more conservative generals, the Ardennes gambit allowed them to slip past Allied defenses and swing north to cut off a vast portion of the Allied armies, sealing the fate of France.

Opposite page: A photo crew from Josef Goebbels's propaganda ministry joins a German advance unit at Dunkirk on May 27, 1940, to take pictures of equipment left on the beach by the defeated British. What escaped their lens was the fact that 198,229 British and 139,997 French soldiers had been evacuated by every ship and boat, large and small, that could be mustered—850 in all. This deft move left the Germans with an empty bag and Britain, under irascible new Prime Minister Churchill, better able to keep up the fight.

Above: As the French army collapses, thousands of *Poilus* are cut off and compelled to surrender. Amid the catastrophe, on June 10, Mussolini declared war on the Allies, and an Italian army invaded Southern France—only to be stopped in its tracks. As the French government fled to Bordeaux, however, German troops entered Paris on June 14.

Left: On June 22, 84-year-old Marshal Philippe Pétain, a World War I hero, signed an armistice that went into effect three days later. The Germans occupied northern France, while the south became the nominally neutral—but tacitly pro-Axis—French State, administered by Pétain from the city of Vichy. In Britain, General Charles de Gaulle rallied a "Free French" army-in-exile to fight on alongside the Allies—and was sentenced to death in absentia by the Vichy government.

Right: The battleship *Lorraine*, one of the few French warships to remain with the Allies after Pétain's capitulation, is shown in Algiers flying American colors on July 4, 1943. On July 3, 1940, the Royal Navy's Force H, including battleships *Valiant* and *Resolution*, battle cruiser *Hood*, and carrier *Ark Royal*, had attacked the Vichy French battle fleet at Mers-el-Kebir near Oran, Algeria, sinking or damaging the capital ships *Brétagne, Dunkerque,* and *Provence* to ensure that the Germans would not use them. "No act was ever more necessary for the life of Britain," Churchill declared, but this same act also stirred French resentment which the Nazi propaganda machine exploited to the fullest.

Below: A Parisian restaurant displays the new policy—closed to Jewish clientele. Split between the occupied north and the Vichy south, the French were equally divided regarding their Jewish population. A shameful number of French citizens turned in their Jewish neighbors for shipment to concentration camps; many others tried to hide them. Thousands more actively resisted, as spies, saboteurs, and later as guides, to help shot-down Allied aircrews evade capture.

Right: German Dornier Do-17Z bombers overfly the English countryside as the Battle of Britain begins in earnest in August 1940. With Churchill of no mind to capitulate, Hitler prepared a plan to invade the island nation. However, for Operation Sea Lion to succeed in the face of the Royal Navy, the Germans needed complete control of the air—which would require the total annihilation of the Royal Air Force.

Left: An RAF pilot awaits the next wave of *Luftwaffe* bombers and their escorts. After the fall of France, German aircraft attacked British Channel shipping and tried—unsuccessfully—to destroy the radar stations that gave the RAF a critical advantage in parrying their aerial thrusts. On August 13, the *Luftwaffe* tried to sweep Fighter Command from the sky, in an operation code-named *Adler Tag* ("Eagle Day"). That, too, failed, but more aerial onslaughts soon followed. For the first time in history, the outcome of a battle, the fate of a nation, and quite possibly the course of the war—was to be decided primarily in the sky.

Above: The front gunner of a Heinkel He-111H scans the sky ahead for trouble as the bombing of Britain continues. Just as the attrition on RAF fighters was reaching the breaking point, Hitler, reacting to a British bombing raid on Germany, ordered the bombing of London, giving RAF Fighter Command a critical reprieve. A major German effort against London on September 15 ended in costly failure, resulting in the date's commemoration in Britain as Battle of Britain Day.

Left: A Hawker Hurricane Mark I sallies forth to meet the German challenge. Most of the RAF fighter force was made up of Hurricanes, which were slower than their more famous stablemates, the Supermarine Spitfires, but were rugged, maneuverable, and easy to maintain and repair. They took a heavy toll on enemy bombers and the occasional German fighter pilot who was bested by a Hurricane was loath to admit it— a phenomenon that German ace Adolf Galland referred to as "Spitfire snobbery."

Right: A Spitfire Mark IIa flown by Flight Lieutenant R. Deacon Elliot of No. 72 Squadron passes over the cliffs of Dover. Ideally, while Hurricanes dealt with German bombers, Spitfires engaged their fighter escorts, easily outfighting the twin-engine Messerschmitt Me-110 *Zerstörer* ("destroyer") and equaling the Me-109E's performance. The "Spit's" principal edge lay in its lower wing loading and consequent ability to outmaneuver the Me-109 in a close turning dogfight, but the outcome of an encounter between these classically well-matched adversaries was usually determined by the skill of the pilot.

Above: An Me-109E pilot suits up for a mission over Britain. Although its fuel-injected Daimler-Benz DB 601 engine gave it some advantages over the Spitfire (the carburetors of the Spitfire's early model Rolls-Royce Merlin engine were prone to choke when inverted or during extreme maneuvers), the Me-109E had only fuel enough for 20 to 30 minutes' flying time over England before being forced to disengage and head for home. That problem was exacerbated by the *Luftwaffe's* change of focus, from eliminating RAF Fighter Command to protecting the bombers—and often their ineffective Me-110 escorts as well!

Above: The dome of St. Paul's Cathedral stands defiantly amid the debris after a bombing raid on London. As daylight attacks became too costly, the Germans switched to bombing by night in an effort to terrorize the British into submission. The British gamely took it in their stride, however, and from late October on the German attacks began to abate. Hitler had written off the prospects of conquering Britain and was turning his attention toward another target—the Soviet Union.

Above: A Spitfire Mark Vc of No. 303 Squadron "Kosciuszko," flown by Flight Sergeant Jan Zumbach, sets off during the cross-Channel duels that followed the Battle of Britain, as the RAF went over to the offensive against German units based in France. First flying Hurricanes, No. 303 Squadron's Polish veterans accounted for the most enemy planes of any RAF unit during the battle—and they went on to show equal zeal in the replacement "Spits." The RAF also had squadrons of expatriate Czechs, Norwegians, Belgians, Dutch, and Free French, as well as three with American volunteers whose nationality was thinly veiled under the sobriquet "Eagle Squadrons."

Right: *Generalmajor* (Brigadier General) Erwin Rommel consults with his *Luftwaffe* commander, *Generalmajor* Stefan Fröhlich, shortly after arriving in Tripoli, Libya, on February 12, 1941. After a desultory invasion of Egypt on September 13, 1940, Italy's large but ill-equipped army was routed by 31,000 counterattacking British troops commanded by Lieutenant General Richard O'Connor who, between December 9, 1940, and January 26, 1941, took 130,000 prisoners and advanced to the outskirts of Tripoli. Hitler reluctantly responded to Mussolini's entreaties for help by sending a small contingent under Rommel, who promptly attacked on March 31, just as the British were withdrawing troops to deal with the imminent German invasion of Greece. By April 10 the British had been thrown back and the port of Tobruk invested for what would be a 242-day siege. Then, on the night of April 6, Lieutenants General O'Connor and Sir Philip Neame were captured near Martuba. Although it was only the beginning of a wildly mobile back-and-forth struggle for North Africa, Rommel and his *Afrika Korps* had already become the stuff of legend.

Above: A Fiat G.50 flies between two Messerschmitt Me-110Ds of *Zerstörergeschwader* (destroyer wing) 26 on patrol, all aircraft marked with the white band that identified Axis aircraft in the North African theater of operations. Conceived in 1936 and entering service in early 1938, the Fiat G.50 *Freccia* (arrow) was the first Italian monoplane fighter with retractable landing gear and an enclosed cockpit. However, due to pilot complaints about the Plexiglas canopy being prone to cracking and too slow to open, the plane was redesigned with an open cockpit.

Opposite page: Commandos undergo training somewhere in England before embarking on any manner of special operations in enemy territory. Delivered and extracted by motor torpedo boat, submarine, airdrop, and a variety of other means, the commandos often inflicted considerable damage, but on July 16, 1940, British Minister of Economic Warfare Hugh Dalton was authorized to go further with a more shadowy organization, the Special Operations Executive. Upon insertion into occupied countries from Norway to Yugoslavia, the SOE worked with resistance groups in the occupied countries to sabotage the German war effort from within, in a dangerous cat-and-mouse game with the Gestapo and other Nazi agencies.

Above: An Me-109E of I *Gruppe, Jagdgeschwader* (fighter wing) 27, attached to *Afrika Korps*, demonstrates the effectiveness of its desert camouflage. Led by Spanish Civil War veteran *Hauptmann* Eduard Neumann I/JG.27, *"Afrika"* took a heavy toll on Allied aircraft and added its own legend to the campaign with Hans-Joachim Marseille, a notoriously ill-disciplined aerial virtuoso whose 158 victories—the highest score for a *Luftwaffe* pilot flying exclusively in the West—included 17 on September 2, 1942. While Marseille was test flying a new Me-109G-1 on September 30, however, smoke from an engine fire filled the cockpit, and as he bailed out he struck his own tailplane and fell to his death.

Right: A Type VIIC *Unterseeboot* in unusual camouflage returns to harbor from an Atlantic sortie. Hopelessly outnumbered by the Royal Navy, the German *Kriegsmarine* pursued a *guerre de course* aimed at choking Britain off from vitally needed supplies by avoiding its warships and sinking its merchant vessels. Occasionally the British eliminated a major warship, most notably *Admiral Graf Spee*, trapped and scuttled in Montevideo harbor, Uruguay, on December 17, 1939, and *Bismarck* on May 26, 1941. Disguised merchant cruisers were harder to hunt down, but the greatest menace was the U-boat, which initially frustrated the destroyers and smaller escort vessels that tried to protect the precious cargo ships.

Left: The Allies' principal counterapproach to the U-boat menace was to gather their ships in convoys, with escort vessels ready to strike whenever the enemy attacked. The U-boats responded by operating in "wolf packs," with squadrons of submarines making coordinated attacks on the convoys from all directions in an attempt to overwhelm the escorts. Convoys were also vulnerable to roving German warships, and disguised merchant cruisers and aircraft, including the long-ranging Focke-Wulf Fw-200C Condor.

Right: Dewoitine D.520Cs stop to refuel at Mertizen, Greece, en route to Vichy-French-controlled Syria in 1941. On April 30, 1941, the Iraqi army, led by pro-German Colonel Ali Rashid al-Gailani, began attacking British forces stationed there, and soon afterward the Germans and Italians sent aircraft, hastily marked in Iraqi insignia, in Ali Rashid's support, staging through Syria. After crushing of the Arab revolt on May 31, Britain sent troops into Syria and Lebanon on June 8. After more than a month of hard fighting the Vichy French surrendered on July 12.

Below: A Panzer III fords a river during Operation Barbarossa, the German invasion of the Soviet Union, which commenced on June 22, 1941. Neither Hitler nor Stalin had any illusions that their August 1939 Non-Aggression Pact had any purpose but to buy time. However, Stalin was so convinced that he would undo the damage his own political purges had done to the Red Army officer corps, and restore it to competitive efficiency before the Germans could attack, that he ignored a succession of warnings that Hitler was about to strike much sooner than expected.

Right: A German motorized unit rolls into Russia. Most of the Soviet air arm was caught on the ground and the survivors shot down by battle-hardened German pilots. The Red Army reeled before the onslaught of 5.5 million Germans in 180 divisions, backed by 47,000 guns, 4,300 tanks, and 5,000 aircraft. Stalin, shaken to discover how thoroughly in denial he had been about the imminent danger, retired to his country *dacha*. For almost two weeks the man who held absolute control over Russia remained virtually incommunicado, leaving the Russian people uncertain as to what they should do.

Below: German infantrymen advance through a Russian town as the general offensive across the steppes continues. "You have only to kick in the door," Hitler had grandly declared of the Soviet Union, "and the whole rotten structure will come crashing down." Events in Barbarossa's first few months seemed to bear out this pronouncement. On July 3, however, Stalin, finally made a radio speech in a low monotone in which he, with uncharacteristic candor, presented the desperate situation and what needed to be done to defend the Motherland. Awkward as it was, it was more effective than Hitlerian bombast could ever have been in galvanizing the people, who were reassured that "the Boss" was back at his post.

Below: While Josef Kiermeier and Karl Wolff look on from left, *Reichsführer* Heinrich Himmler selects a Russian boy for deportation to Germany, so that his "racially valuable traits" can be studied. This boy's ultimate fate is unknown, but he could have been subjected to medical experimentation, sent to a slave labor camp, or killed outright. Typically, a POW determined to be a Communist party member, a political commissar, or a Jew would have been shot or sent to a concentration camp. For thousands of Russians, who might otherwise have regarded the Germans as liberators from Stalin's oppressive rule, the racial ideology at Nazism's core was more effective than Soviet propaganda at turning the struggle into a "Great Patriotic War."

Above right: German infantry sweep a street in a Russian town, backed up by a *Panzer Abwehr Kanone* (antitank gun) 37. A mainstay of the German army at the start of the war, the PAK 37 was also mounted on its main battle tank, the Panzer III. The Germans, however, soon discovered the 37mm shell to be inadequate against the Soviet heavy and medium tanks they encountered in growing numbers from July 1941 on, leading to their dismissively referring to the gun as the "Doorknocker" and desperately calling for newer, heavier, better-penetrating antitank weaponry.

Right: German motorcycle dispatch riders find themselves in the awkwardly ironic position of having to dig their vehicle out of a Russian road that has become a morass of mud. The *Wehrmacht's* swift advances over the Russian steppes in the summer of 1941 ground to a frustrating crawl that autumn, as rains brought the unanticipated intervention of "General Mud" into the scenario. Nevertheless, driven by memories of the debacle that had befallen Napoleon's invasion of Russia in 1812, Hitler urged his forces forward in a critical race to take Moscow before winter set in.

Above: German soldiers examine early model T-34/76 medium tanks that had become bogged down in the marshes near Tolochin. Although often ineptly used by their crews and unit commanders in the campaign's early months, the 28-ton T-34 caused profound concern in the German high command, who were impressed by its outstanding combination of an efficient, reliable 500-hp diesel engine, simple Christie suspension with wide treads for mobility, 33mph (53kph) speed, angled armor that was 4 inches (10cm) thick, and a good, versatile 76.2mm gun—its principal weakness being cramped quarters for four crewmen. As easy to mass-produce as it was to maintain, later upgraded with an 85mm gun in an enlarged turret, the T-34 would ultimately play a vital role in Soviet victory.

Opposite page: A 150mm heavy artillery piece adds its punch to the German effort outside Moscow, but the *Wehrmacht* has stalled, and as the Russian winter becomes harsher the inadequacies of the clothing issued to them begin to take a toll on the German soldiers. The Germans managed to come within sight of the Moscow skyline before December 6, 1941, when Soviet counterattacks suddenly threw them back on a wide front. Although the Germans managed to stop the drive and even regain some ground, both Hitler and Churchill recognized the precedent set by this first major defeat of a German army on land since the war had begun. An equally significant event occurred the next day, as the hitherto-neutral United States was suddenly, forcibly, plunged into the conflict.

Above: As Panzer IIIs continue their seemingly inexorable advance on Moscow in October 1941, colder weather restores their mobility. Still, despite its horrendous losses—including 310,000 who were taken prisoner in a grand encirclement east of Smolensk between July 16 and August 8—the Red Army continued to regroup and resist. Meanwhile, learning through Richard Sorge (a spy in Germany's Tokyo embassy), that Japan was planning to attack the Western powers in the Far East, Stalin decided to transfer Siberian troops guarding the Mongolian border to Moscow—and with them General Georgy Zhukov.

Right: US Navy sailors pay their respects to some of the 2,404 Americans killed at Pearl Harbor. Besides drawing an outraged United States into the conflict, the Pearl Harbor raid forced the Americans to revise their naval tactics around the capital ships that had completely escaped destruction in the raid: aircraft carriers. Besides failing to catch any flattops in the harbor, the Japanese failed to destroy any of the four submarines berthed there or set fire to the fuel tanks at Pearl Harbor.

Below: US Army riflemen and canine film star Rin Tin Tin demonstrate the use of gas masks during a staged exercise. Although all sides were prepared for it, chemical warfare never saw significant use on any battlefield during World War II. It is not hard to understand why Hitler was loath to resort to it—he had been a victim of mustard gas in 1918. The Nazis would have less compunction, however, about using poison gas on the mostly civilian inmates of their concentration camps.

Above: A US Army soldier, armed with an M-1 Garand rifle, trains alongside an M-3 halftrack. A major innovation among armies still armed with bolt-action rifles, the semiautomatic M-1 Garand was also reliable and accurate, and it became the mainstay of the American infantryman. It took somewhat longer for the Marines in the Pacific to overcome their reluctance to part with their bolt-action M-1903 Springfields, which even after the adoption of the Garand they often kept for use as sniper rifles.

Right: For roughly half a year after Pearl Harbor, Japanese forces swiftly overran the Philippines, Malaya, Singapore, Burma, the Dutch East Indies, and Hong Kong, while continuing their advance into China. Even while his Nationalist army reeled under a series of defeats, however, Generalissimo Chiang Kai-shek moved his government to the mountain city of Chungking in central western China, while to the north his Communist rival Mao Tse-tung fought a guerrilla war against the Japanese in the countryside.

Below: Aiding Chiang Kai-shek was a fighter unit of mercenary adventurers called the American Volunteer Group (AVG). Under the brilliant tactical leadership of Colonel Claire L. Chennault, the "Flying Tigers" claimed an astounding 229 aerial victories and a total of 297 enemy planes destroyed for the loss of 21 men killed or captured. In mid-May 1942, eight of its aircraft drove the Japanese 53rd Division back from the Salween River Gorge, preventing it from invading China from the south. On July 4, 1942, the AVG was assimilated into the US Army Air Forces as the 23rd Fighter Group, forming the nucleus for what ultimately became the Fourteenth Air Force.

Chapter 3

Doing Their Bit

Opposite page: Women workers lunch under the shade of camouflage netting at the Consolidated-Vultee plant in July 1943, with PB2Ys nearing completion in the background. Intended as a successor to Consolidated's PBY-5A Catalina, the PB2Y's range of 1,070 miles (1,722km)—compared to the PBY's 2,520—rendered it less suitable for long-range maritime patrol work and only 217 were built. Its size and capacity, however, made it a useful cargo and troop carrier, and it was extensively used by the Naval Air Transport Service.

Maximum effort—total war. The concepts were far from new when World War II broke out, but never had so large a percentage of combatant nations' populations been involved, to the extent that even an act of personal frugality could be deemed vital to the war effort. The British called it "doing your bit," and every subject was encouraged to do his or her part.

The home front war mobilized a patriotic spirit in most citizens, a spirit that had already shown itself during the Great Depression. It also raised contradictions and sowed the seeds of social change. Adolf Hitler had promised work for every German in a revived economy, but as the war ground on and more men were conscripted into military service, German manpower became insufficient to sustain the war machine, leading the military to rely increasingly on slave labor drawn from the "subhumans" in the concentration camps.

In Britain and the United States, women took on a wide array of traditionally male tasks behind the lines, freeing the men for frontline service. In so doing, they acquired a new perspective on their abilities and place in society. Arguably, the exigencies of war shook up Japan even more, as women also took on roles previously unthinkable in the traditional hierarchy that coexisted with 20th-century technology. Black American men and women, too, took on responsibilities long denied them and likewise found it a lot harder to go back to the "separate but unequal" arrangement under which they had lived.

Besides working in factories and rear echelon jobs, thousands of Soviet women fought at the front, including in three all-female air regiments. Two pilots, Lidya Litvyak and Ekaterina Budanova, became history's only female fighter aces before both fell in combat. The precedent they set would blaze a trail for the first women in space.

Below: A German metal worker machines a part in a wartime factory. During the heady victories of 1939 and '40, the Nazi government demanded relatively few sacrifices at home but, soon, widening battlefronts and the failure to take Moscow in 1941 made it clear that swift ultimate victory was not to be. Making up for lost time, Albert Speer mobilized the German people for a war effort on a par with that of their allied counterparts, with the controversial addition of slave labor drawn from concentration camps—a program designed to achieve both production and extermination by literally working the "racially inferior" laborers to death.

Right: A Civil Defence Warden inspects damage to buildings in London's Holborn district. Initially regarded as a nuisance for their constant admonishments to civilians to black out their houses at night, the wardens attained heroic stature during the Battle of Britain. In that historic event, they guided people to shelters and remaining above ground to help any stragglers throughout the bombing raids, after which they were among the first to administer first aid, put out small fires and assess bomb damage.

Left: Two members of the Royal Observer Corps watch the Channel from a cliff-side position. First formed on October 29, 1925, the Observer Corps consisted of civilians who received mobilization notices on August 24, 1939, and, in their spare time, remained on continuous duty from then until May 12, 1945. Reporting to Royal Air Force Command Groups and Sector Control, the observers helped in tracking and plotting enemy air attacks, and in issuing timely air raid warnings that saved countless lives during the 1940 London Blitz—and again during the V-1 guided bomb attacks in 1944.

Above: Auxiliary Territorial Service members help guard the Channel coast by working at the plotting table of 428 Battery, Coast Defence Artillery. For the purposes of passing the censor for publication on December 21, 1942, much of the plotting table was covered over and a false coastline drawn on the map before the photo was taken. Formed on September 9, 1938, the ATS was a branch of the British Army for all women volunteers except medical and dental officers and nurses. ATS members received two-thirds the pay of a man of equivalent rank.

Right: A nurse tends to evacuees from Plymouth in the garden of the Chaim Weizmann Home at Tapley Park, Instow, North Devon, in October 1942. Britain began planning for the possible need to relocate people from endangered areas near the south coast and in the cities with Operation Pied Piper on September 1, 1939. Relocations—particularly of children—to homes and facilities in the countryside began in earnest during the Battle of Britain and the bombing of London, when some 25,000 families lost their homes. The evacuations peaked at 1.37 million people in February 1941.

Below: A sailor stationed at Naval Air Station Quonset Point, Rhode Island, watches a WREN ceremoniously remove the US Navy star off a Grumman F4F Wildcat to reveal the Fleet Air Arm roundel beneath. Peaking at 74,620 in 1944, the Women's Royal Naval Service or "WRENs" encompassed pilots of the Air Transport Auxiliary, whose various duties included ferrying Lend-Lease aircraft from the United States to Britain. Not in direct combat but by no means out of harm's way, 102 WRENs were killed and 22 wounded in the course of the war.

Above: Munitions workers learn to fire a mortar under army supervision near the English coast on December 31, 1942. Even after the cancellation of Operation Sea Lion at the end of 1940, the British were reminded of the need for constant vigilance and readiness, as on February 11–13, 1942, when the German battle cruisers *Scharnhorst* and *Gneisenau* and heavy cruiser *Prinz Eugen* departed Brest and slipped up the Channel to German ports under the embarrassed noses of Coastal Command. The female British factory workers never got to fire weapons in anger, but their Russian counterparts in Leningrad and Stalingrad often did.

Below: A cargo of flour from the United States and Canada is unloaded from a merchant ship in Britain. No civilians among the Western Allies put themselves in more continuous danger than merchant seamen on the North Atlantic between 1940 and 1943, but Britain could not have sustained itself without them. In the case of the US Merchant Marine, which began the war with 55,000 personnel and peaked at 215,000, 1,554 ships were sunk and 9,300 seamen (one man out of every 26) were killed—yet the US government did not officially recognize them as veterans until 1988.

Right: "War news" has relatively low priority among the headlines displayed outside the *Brockton Enterprise* in Brockton, Massachusetts, in December 1940. For the first year of the war, the America First Committee's opposition to President Roosevelt's notions of involving the United States was supported by Republicans, agrarian progressives such as William Jennings Bryan and Robert M. La Follette, Irish immigrants with antipathy toward Britain, and German-American Bundists sympathetic to Hitler. That began to change in 1940, as Hitler's conquests in Europe spread public anxieties about a Western hemisphere menaced by hostile powers across both the Atlantic and Pacific oceans.

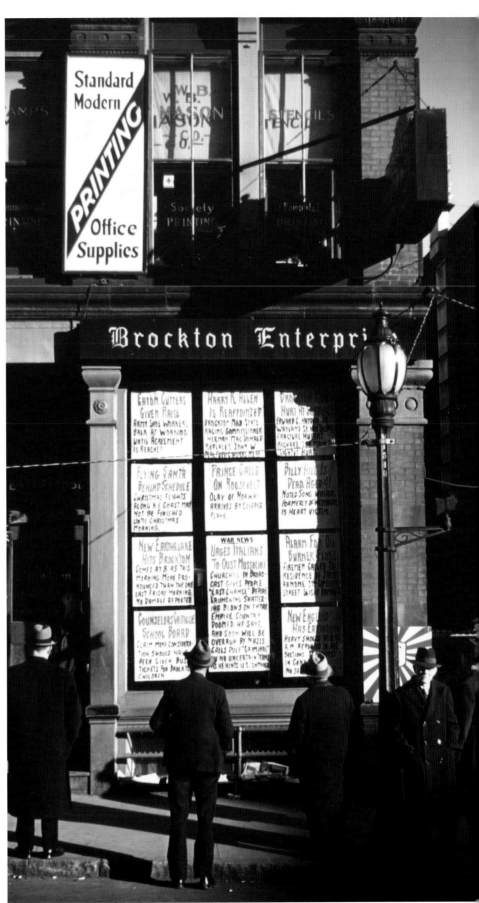

Left: A factory employee at the Goodyear Rubber and Tire Company in Akron, Ohio, works on a self-sealing fuel tank for an airplane in December 1941. Even before the United States entered the war, its military was undergoing a modernization program and many of its products were being shipped to Britain through the Lend-Lease Program. "Neutrality Patrols," in which US Navy ships escorted Atlantic and Caribbean convoys as far east as Iceland, led to incidents that climaxed on October 31, 1941, when the German U-552 sank the destroyer *Reuben James* with 111 of its 159-man crew.

Above: The Japanese "sneak attack" on Pearl Harbor, on December 7, 1941, prompted the United States to begin fighting in the war, literally with a vengeance on the part of an outraged populace. Virginia Young (right), whose husband was among the first to die at Pearl Harbor, became a supervisor in the assembly and repairs department at Naval Air Station Corpus Christi, Texas, arranging for the provision of living quarters for out-of-state workers such as electric drill operator Ethel Mann, at left.

Above: A Bessemer converter, turning iron into steel at the Allegheny Ludlum Steel Corp. in Brackenridge, Pennsylvania, strains to satisfy a rapidly growing need as American manufacture gears up for total war. In 1943, US steel production came to 80.6 million tons (73 million tonnes), compared to 13.2 million in Britain, 8.5 million in the Soviet Union, 34.6 million in Germany and the countries it occupied, and 6.3 million in Japan.

Above: A welder at the Combustion Engineering Company, an innovative engineering firm that employed 30,000 employees in a dozen states at its peak of activity, produces a ship's boiler at its Chattanooga, Tennessee, plant in June 1942. During the war American ship production outstripped all others, with 22 aircraft carriers (compared to 14 British and 16 Japanese), plus 141 escorts converted from merchantmen, as well as eight battleships, 48 cruisers, 349 destroyers, 420 escort vessels, 203 submarines (surpassed only by the Germans, with 1,141), and almost 34 million tons of merchant shipping.

Left: A member of a construction crew at Fort Knox, Kentucky, unloads wiring prior to erecting a new 33,000-volt electric power line in June 1942. As the army facility there expanded to accommodate thousands of new trainees, the need for a supplement to its existing electric power was anticipated by the connection of a new power line to a new hydroelectric plant at the nearby city of Louisville.

Below: In the spring of 1942, food rationing was instituted in the United States, limiting civilian food and fuel purchases through a system of ration cards. To supplement their diet—and often to contribute more food for the troops—many civilians grew their own food in "Victory Gardens" and became adept at home canning, as exemplified here. A darker side effect of rationing was the emergence of illegal selling of commodities at inflated prices through the black market.

Opposite page: Children stage a patriotic demonstration in Southington, Connecticut, in May 1942. Completing the American public's transition from an isolationist mindset to a total war mentality, wartime propaganda reached deep into the psyche using media of all sorts, including animated cartoons from the major studios. Walt Disney showed Donald Duck having a nightmare of living under Nazism in *Der Führer's Face*; Warner Brothers had Bugs Bunny bedeviled by a gremlin and in turn bedeviling Hermann Göring in the Black Forest; Dave Fleischer's *Superman* rooted out Nazi spies and "Japateurs"; and Max Fleischer's Popeye—naturally—went to sea to take on the Japanese navy.

Above: Among the most-emphasized means by which civilians not directly involved in the military or war-related production could contribute to victory was conservation. In October 1942, Annette del Sur, wearing an aluminum crown as "Salvage Queen" of the Douglas Aircraft Company in Long Beach, California, publicized her plant's participation in the nationwide campaign to contribute scrap metal to the war effort.

Left: Rural school children in San Augustine County, Texas, study geography in April 1943 with a keen interest that they'd never had before. American commitments overseas spread an unprecedented profusion of exotic names across the front pages of the country's newspapers, generating curiosity about the foreign locales where US troops were fighting. In one case of astute timing, Warner Brothers moved up the premiere of its cinematic combination of propaganda and romance, *Casablanca*, to November 26, 1942, just weeks after Operation Torch had emblazoned that Moroccan city in the news media.

Left: Patriotism had its darker side. In the wake of Pearl Harbor, in February 1942 the Roosevelt administration, deeming the American West Coast vulnerable, ordered the relocation of Americans of Japanese descent to internment camps such as the Tule Lake Relocation Center at Newell, California. Few challenged the incarceration of some 100,000 Japanese-Americans, which was ostensibly for their own "protection." Thousands of suspect German and Italian Americans were also incarcerated, and 58,000 Italian-Americans voluntarily complied with orders to relocate from "strategic" areas on the California coast. Following his reelection in November 1944, Roosevelt canceled the "War Emergency Evacuation" and closed the camps.

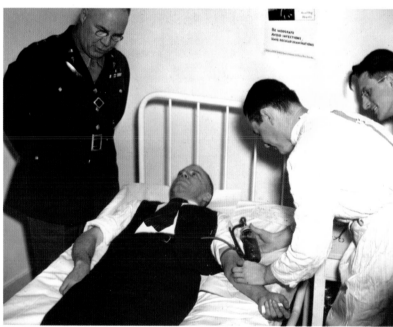

Above: Robert Patterson, Undersecretary of War, makes a very personal contribution at a blood reception depot in the Pentagon Building, jointly operated by the American Red Cross and the Army Medical Center, outside of Washington, D.C., in February 1943. Major General James C. McGee, the surgeon general, looks on at left while Captain John Reichen takes a pint that may very well save a soldier's life at the front.

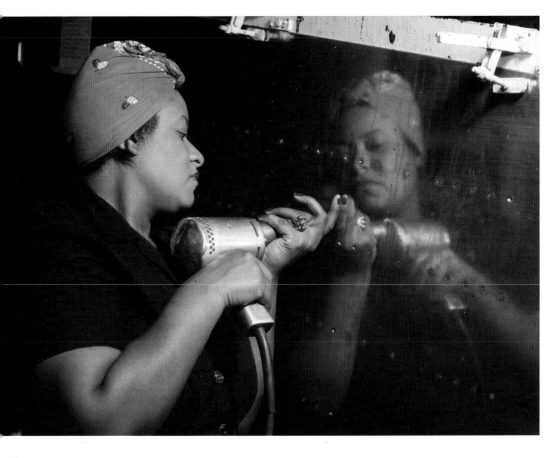

Left: "Rosie the Riveter" became an iconic symbol of the American woman, empowered by patriotism, giving her utmost for victory. This worker, however, drilling rivet holes in the side of a Vengeance dive bomber at a subcontracting Vultee factory in Nashville, Tennessee in February 1943, represents a further change in the established order—she is African American. As was the case with the black soldiers who served on the front lines, the end of the conflict would see her unwilling to return her former prewar place within a less-than-equal social order in the "Land of the Free."

Below: Female workers at the Consolidated-Vultee Aircraft Factory at Downey, California, wire the electrical equipment on a PB2Y Coronado patrol bomber in July 1943. Representing a newer wartime generation of warplanes, the Coronado was a large and extremely complex piece of machinery, although Boeing's B-29 bomber outdid it as arguably the most complicated article of aerial technology devised during the war.

Opposite page: Two workers complete assembly of a Pratt and Whitney R-2800 Double Wasp engine, probably in preparation for its installation in an F4U-1 Corsair, at the Vought-Sikorsky Aircraft Factory in Stratford, Connecticut, in March 1943. Introduced in 1939, the 18-cylinder air-cooled radial proved to be as rugged and reliable as it was powerful, generating 2,000hp, later upgraded to 2,800hp for short spurts, with water injection. Among the aircraft it propelled to glory were the Corsair, Grumman F6f Hellcat, Republic P-47 Thunderbolt, Martin B-26 Marauder, and Douglas A-26 Intruder.

Above: Viola Sievers, a wiper who was her mother's sole source of support and had a son-in-law in the Army, cleans off a giant "H" class locomotive with a blast of live steam at the roundhouse in Clinton, Iowa. The diversion of war materials to other priorities stopped the building of new diesel-electric locomotives during World War II, as a consequence of which steam locomotives were used more extensively than ever before.

Left: Women employed as engine wipers, generally cleaning 12 locomotives a day, take their lunch break in the roundhouse at Clinton, Iowa. Although the amount of track, nationwide, had declined to 226,000 miles (361,000km) from 254,000 (406,000km) during World War I, more-powerful engines and the development of diesel-electric locomotives increased the net tonnage the average train could transport. The most efficient form of mass land transport, troop trains introduced a new generation of young Americans to rail travel.

Below: The badge worn by this garage mechanic in Newark, New Jersey, photographed in December 1943, identified him as a member of the Office of Defense Transportation. Established by President Roosevelt on December 18, 1941, the ODT's mission was to "assume maximum utilization of the domestic transportation facilities of the Nation for the successful prosecution of the war." In practice, this involved coordinating stateside car and rail transport to ensure that transporting of war materials to the front had priority over "nonessential" activities.

Above: An employee of the Electric Boat Company of Groton, Connecticut, wearing his shipyard security clearance badge on his hat, was photographed by Edward Steichen as he worked on the hull of the submarine *Blenny* (SS-324) in the summer of 1943. Launched on April 9, 1944, and entering combat on November 10, *Blenny* completed four patrols off Java and in the South China Sea, sinking eight Japanese cargo ships, along with 62 smaller craft, using its deck guns.

Below: Corporal Beth Haddow and Private First Class Dorothy Hamilton pose before a Transportation Corps flag for a recruitment poster. Thousands of Women's Army Corps (WAC) personnel were assigned to the Transportation Corps to expedite the shipping of men and materiel. In addition, they processed "V-mail," in which morale-boosting letters to and from overseas personnel were photographed on microfilm, allowing vast quantities of it to be transported and then enlarged at its destination.

Right: Specialists (Transportation) Third Class Dorothy Knee and Genevieve Close direct aircraft arrivals and departures from the tower at Naval Air Station Anacostia, District of Columbia, in mid-1943. After 23 years of nurses being the only female naval personnel, the first Women Accepted for Volunteer Emergency Service (WAVES) enlistee entered US Navy service in early August 1942. By the end of the year, 8,000 naval officers were women and ten times that number of enlisted women were engaged in a far wider variety of roles than they had done before.

Right: A WAVE instructor gives pointers to an officer checking out a Link Army Navy Trainer Model 18 (ANT-18) at Naval Air Station Norfolk, Virginia. Invented by Edwin Albert Link in 1929, the basic instrument simulator used an electric pump to provide a realistic pitch and roll response to the controls. Ten thousand ANT-18s, nicknamed "Blue Boxes," were built and some 500,000 pilots were introduced to flight in them before going on to real aircraft.

Below: Jean Selby, a WAVE attached to the Photographic Laboratory at Naval Air Station Anacostia, makes celluloid transparencies for a training film on deep sea diving. Many of the WAVES involved in film production for the Navy had been illustrators at Walt Disney Studios, applying their entertainment techniques toward creating an informative as well as lively, and thereby memorable, training film.

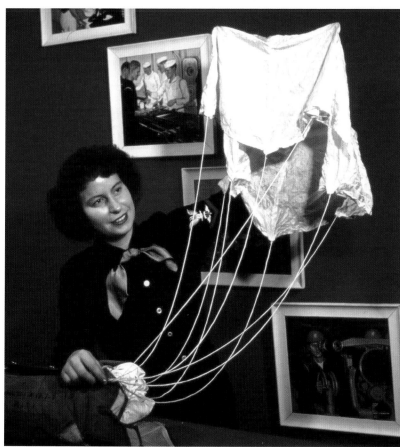

Above: A WAVE parachute rigger holds up the pilot chute during a demonstration of parachute packing tools and techniques at Naval Air Station New York. Connected to the main parachute by a bridle, the auxiliary pilot chute was the first to catch the wind, at which point it would pull out and deploy the main chute. Needless to say, lives depended on the rigger packing the parachute correctly.

Below: Second Lieutenant Louise Matchett, a WAC medical department physical therapist, prepares to administer a short wave diathermy treatment in the Physical Therapy Department, Convalescent Section of the Walter Reed General Hospital at Forest Glen, Maryland, in 1945. Even after the fighting was over, medical personnel in all the armed forces had much to do as the wounded and injured casualties of war needed to be healed and helped in making their transition back into the peacetime world.

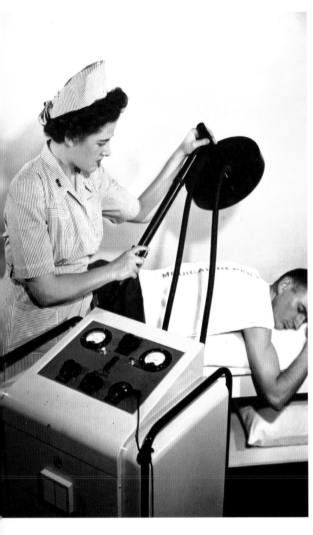

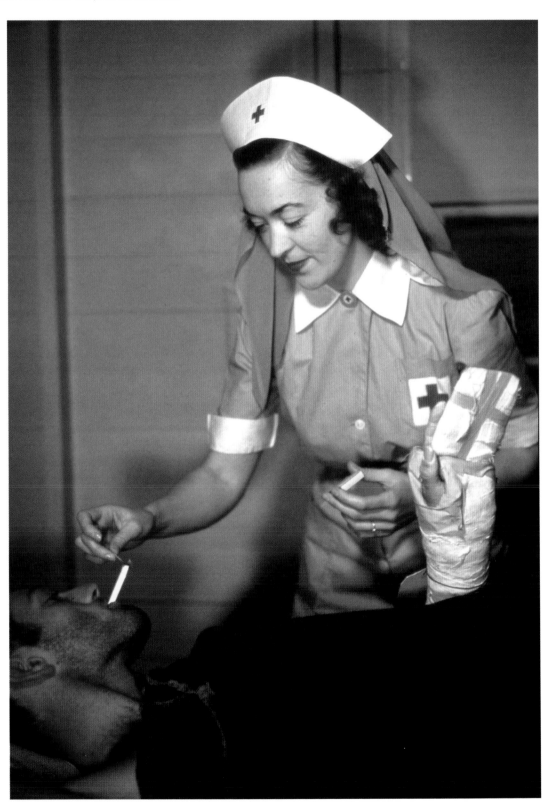

Right: Mrs. R. D. Whitley, a Red Cross volunteer "Grey Lady," lights a cigarette for Construction Mechanic Third Class Ralph Haynes at the Air Evacuation Center at Naval Air Station Patuxent River, Maryland, in 1945. The injured Seabee had arrived after a 14-hour flight from Oakland, California, on the Naval Air Transport Service's "Hospital Express." From NAS Patuxent, a small NATS plane flew him to Washington for admission to the Bethesda Medical Center.

Below: A seamstress repairs an American flag at the Charleston Navy Yard, South Carolina, in 1945. Easily overlooked, the professional descendents of Betsy Ross performed prosaic but essential service throughout the war in keeping the service personnel clothed and their uniforms repaired and maintained. Flags were an important means of communication and identification in all the navies—as well as the logical items to wave in celebration when the fighting was over at last.

Above: Jane Kandeigh, one of the first Navy Flight Nurses to fly to or from an active battlefield in the Pacific, poses for the camera on the wing of a Douglas R5D—the Navy version of the C-54 Skymaster—on Okinawa in late April 1945. The first 24 graduates of the Navy Flight Nurse School at Naval Air Station Alameda, California, in January 1945, could swim a mile, tow or push a victim for 220 yards (201m), and swim 440 yards (402m) in 10 minutes.

Chapter 4

Reversal of Fortunes

Opposite page: German motorized troops are ferried across a river. On July 23, German forces secured Rostov and on July 25 they began crossing the Don River to begin the push toward Stalingrad. On August 9, Army Group A reached the foothills of the Caucasus, having advanced 300 miles (482km) in two weeks. By August 20 the Germans had taken Maikop and were poised to take the Black Sea Coast, with the prize oil cities of Grozny and Baku.

Despite German failures to seize Moscow and Tobruk, some British successes at sea—most notably the sinking of the battleship *Bismarck* on May 26—and the Italian losses of their colonies Ethiopia and Somaliland, 1941 had been a bleak year for the Allies, and 1942 started out bleaker, with U-boats slaughtering American merchant ships and the Japanese overrunning Hong Kong, Malaya, Singapore, Burma, the Dutch East Indies, the Philippines, and northern New Guinea with stunning swiftness. Heavy-handed Soviet counterattacks and British attempts to defeat Rommel ended in costly failure.

An ingenious attack on Japan by carrier-launched medium bombers on April 18 boosted American morale, and in May the US Navy repulsed a Japanese invasion force in the Battle of the Coral Sea. The first real turning point, however, came in June, when American dive bombers sank four Japanese fleet carriers near Midway. Following up that victory, US Marines landed on Guadalcanal on August 7. After six months of savage fighting on land, air, and sea, the island was secured in February 1943.

In North Africa, Rommel defeated an Anglo-French army at Gazala and went on to take Tobruk on June 21. In Russia, the Germans launched a new offensive aimed at seizing oil fields in the Caucasus Mountains, as well as the Volga River city of Stalingrad. In the Caucasus, the Red Army's fighting retreat ultimately stalled the German advance. At Stalingrad, a stubborn defense also brought the German Sixth Army to a standstill, after which, on November 19, a Soviet counteroffensive began its encirclement.

Keen to follow up his recent successes with further achievements, Rommel invaded Egypt in July, only to be stopped and then thrown back at El Alamein. At that point, Allied landings in Morocco and Algeria in November left Rommel and his army struggling for survival in Tunisia.

Above: Rommel allegedly took this photograph of vehicles advancing in North Africa—if so, he presumably shot it outside of Tripoli, beyond which they would have had to run a gauntlet of Allied aircraft or marauding raiders such as the British Army's Special Air Service. Late in 1941 a British offensive, Operation Crusader, had driven Rommel back to El Agheila, but, after receiving reinforcements, he launched a reconnaissance in force against the overstretched British on January 21, which led to his retaking Benghazi on January 28 and Timimi on February 3. The next day, he was halted along a 50-mile (80km) line of defensive "boxes" established between Gazala, 30 miles (48km) west of Tobruk, and Bir Hakeim to the south.

Left: In February 1942 the US Navy launched a series of raids—primarily making use of its principal punch, aircraft carriers—to harass Japanese bases throughout the Pacific. While approaching the Japanese naval and air base at Rabaul on February 20, 1942, carrier Lexington came under attack from 17 Mitsubishi G4M1 twin-engine bombers, but Grumman F4F-3 Wildcats of the ship's fighter squadron VF-3 shot down or severely damaged all but two of them. Five of these were credited to Lieutenant Edward H. "Butch" O'Hare, making him the US Navy's first ace of the war and earning him the Medal of Honor.

Below: Appointed US Army Chief of Staff on September 1, 1939, General George Catlett Marshall faced the prodigious task of transforming an ill-equipped army of 189,000 men into a trained fighting force that, as of December 7, 1941, would have to fight overseas on at least two fronts. A superb organizer, he largely managed to accomplish that goal with the help of Lieutenant General Leslie McNair, although their individual replacement system for rotating troops in and out of the 90 divisions sometimes broke down. Marshall's choice of commanders was equally mixed, ranging from poor, like Lloyd Fredendall, to controversial, like Mark Clark, to outstanding, such as Dwight D. Eisenhower and Omar Bradley.

Opposite page: *Luftwaffe* ground crewmen dig a Junkers Ju-87B Stuka out of the snow for a mission on the Arctic front in early 1942. Since the full investment of Leningrad in September 8, 1941, much of their effort was devoted to bombing the city and thwarting any attempts to bring sustenance to its populace until November 20, when the Red Army established the so-called "Road of Life" across frozen Lake Ladoga. That hazardous route was Leningrad's only source of supplies until a more substantial corridor was carved out, on January 13, 1943. A Soviet counteroffensive finally lifted the 872-day siege on January 27, 1944, by which time more than a million Russian soldiers had been killed, captured, or were missing, and 642,000 civilians had died in the city. Another 400,000 civilians were slain during evacuation efforts. Among those evacuated on October 1, 1941, was composer Dmitri Shostakovich, who dedicated his Symphony no. 7 in C Major, op. 60, to Leningrad upon its debut at Kuibyshev on March 5, 1942.

Left: *Kapitänleutnant* Reinhard "Teddy" Suhren—who maintained that the only way to get proper rest was in his pajamas—catches some sleep aboard the conning tower of *U-564* while on Caribbean patrol. As the U-boats turned on Germany's new enemy, American inexperience and negligence gave them their second "Happy Time" since their early run of success against the British, as submarines prowled the US coast, torpedoing merchant ships within sight of their own ports. In this, its seventh patrol of the war, *U-564* sank five ships between July 9 and September 18. In its previous visit to American waters between April 4 and June 6, it had sunk four ships and damaged two.

Left: The bridge watch aboard *U-564* scans the horizon as it returns to Brest on September 18. Even in such seemingly safe home waters vigilance was essential. *U-564*, now under Hans Fiedler, was departing on its 12th patrol as part of a five-boat wolf pack when a Short Sunderland of No. 228 Squadron attacked it in the Bay of Biscay on September 13, 1943. Antiaircraft gunners shot down the flying boat, but 28 Germans were killed and *U-564* was damaged. As *U-185* towed it back to Brest the next day, an Armstrong-Whitworth Whitley of Coastal Command's Tenth Operational Training Unit attacked them, was also shot down, and its crew taken prisoner, but not before inflicting enough damage for Fiedler and 17 surviving crewmen to be evacuated and *U-564* scuttled.

Above: A k-type Blimp patrols over an American convoy. Capable of loitering over the merchant-men longer than maritime patrol planes could, the very presence of the US Navy's nonrigid airships was often enough to discourage U-boats from attacking, lest they spot one and call in a lethal response from warships or aircraft. Equally unsung were civilian-flown planes of the Civil Air Patrol, which also patrolled US coastal waters to report any sign of submarine activity—and even occasionally attacked them with bombs.

Left: After five months of intoxicating successes, Japan received a rude shock on April 18, 1942, when 16 North American B-25B bombers, launched from the aircraft carrier Hornet, struck at Tokyo and five other cities in the Home Islands, doing little material damage but significantly affecting Japanese morale. The planner and leader of this calculated risk, Lieutenant Colonel James H. Doolittle, landed in China and with Chinese help made his way back to the United States, where he was awarded the Medal of Honor. He was put in successive command of the Twelfth, Fifteenth, and Eighth Air forces, ending the war as a lieutenant general.

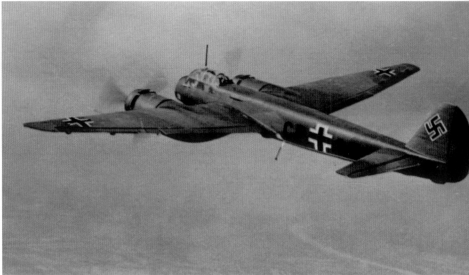

Above: Supermarine Seafires, adapted for oceanic operations, assemble on the deck of a British carrier in 1942. On April 13, 1942, standard Spitfire Mark Vbs took off from *USS Wasp* to reinforce the beleaguered air defenses on the small but strategically vital isle of Malta, followed by a second Spitfire contingent from *Wasp* and British carrier *Eagle* on May 9. Prior to those deliveries, Malta had fended off Italian and German efforts to neutralize its sea and air facilities with a handful of Gloster Gladiator biplanes, later joined by Hawker Hurricanes. Despite relentless air attacks and a succession of supply convoys, Malta held out and did much to disrupt Axis efforts to supply their forces in North Africa.

Above right: A Junkers Ju-88A departs on a mission over the Mediterranean Sea in 1942. Designed as a medium bomber with dive-bombing capabilities, the versatile Ju-88 served in numerous other roles in the course of its long career, including night fighter and remote-controlled flying bomb. Ju-88s took a horrific toll on British warships off Crete during the German airborne invasion of that island in May 1941, and they struck at Malta and the convoys striving to supply it throughout 1942.

Right: As chief of RAF Bomber Command, Air Marshal Sir Arthur Harris embarked on an increasingly ambitious program to repay the destruction and terror the Germans had dealt Britain many times over. On the night of May 30, he launched the first "Thousand Plane Raid" on Cologne, also making use of a continuous "bomber stream" of successive waves of squadrons to overwhelm the German radar and night fighter defenses.

Above: Bombs are loaded aboard an Avro Lancaster. Britain's first four-engine bomber, the Short Stirling, turned out to be inadequate for Harris's bombing effort, but the Lancaster— a four-engine version of the unsuccessful twin-engine Manchester—proved to be one of the best strategic bombers of the war and served RAF Bomber Command throughout, alongside a competent supplemental stablemate, the Handley-Page Halifax. The Lancaster's generous bomb bay could carry prodigious loads, including the 22,000-pound (9,979kg) Grand Slam, the largest and most powerful non-nuclear bomb delivered by an airplane.

Left: A Canadian airman of RAF Bomber Command suits up for a mission aboard his Lancaster in 1942. Avro Canada built its own version of the Lancaster, the B Mark X, for Royal Canadian Air Force squadrons operating from British bases. An additional 15 RCAF squadrons operated Halifaxes under RAF Bomber Command. Canadian pilots distinguished themselves in all other warplanes fielded by the RAF and RCAF. Their ranks included the highest scoring of Malta's defenders, Spitfire pilot George Buerling, who downed 27 Axis planes in 14 days out of his wartime total of 31⅓.

Right: Panzer IVs pass a disabled, abandoned British Universal carrier during a desert battle. On May 26, Rommel struck at the Gazala Line. He also tried to flank it from the south by taking Bir Hakeim, but its Free French Foreign Legion defenders—whose ranks included many expatriate German Jews—stubbornly held, while to the north Rommel's forces were surrounded in an enclave called the Cauldron. Although hard pressed, Rommel ultimately broke out, forcing his Eighth Army opponent, Major General Neil Ritchie, to abandon Gazala on June 14, and consequently compelling the French to evacuate Bir Hakeim. Rommel capped off the most remarkable victory of his career by finally capturing Tobruk on June 21. Promoted to field marshal, the "Desert Fox" set his sights on Egypt and the Suez Canal.

Left: Two US Navy sailors get some bunk time between battles. In the Battle of the Coral Sea on May 4–7, 1942, the US Navy sank Japanese light carrier *Shoho* but lost carrier *Lexington* as well as destroyer *Sims* and tanker *Neosho*, a tactical defeat that nevertheless turned back an invasion force bound for Port Moresby, New Guinea. On June 4, Japanese carrier fighters decimated waves of American bombers from Midway Island and torpedo planes from three carriers, but in so doing they left their ships vulnerable to dive bombers from *Yorktown* and *Enterprise*, which in four minutes inflicted fatal damage to carriers *Akagi, Kaga* and *Soryu*. Subsequent fighting cost the Americans *Yorktown* and destroyer *Hammann*, but the Japanese lost their carrier *Hiryu* and heavy cruiser *Mikuma*, in their first major naval defeat in 350 years.

Right: German soldiers—joined by some local Ukrainian women—take in a theatrical production somewhere on the Eastern Front in the summer of 1942. Having weathered a series of mishandled Soviet counteroffensives throughout the winter and spring, the *Wehrmacht* was reorganized for a new ambitious plan from the *Führer: Fall Blau* (Case Blue), an offensive aimed at seizing Soviet oil fields in the Caucasus and Caspian Sea regions.

Below: Crewmen of a halftrack personnel carrier clean their vehicle in preparation for the next advance—or possibly in anticipation of an order for a brand new paint job. During 1942, the field-gray finish of the *Wehrmacht's* earlier days gave way to a more sophisticated camouflage pattern involving a basic yellow tan covered with various-size blotches of green, brown or both, depending on the terrain.

Opposite page: A German flamethrower eliminates a well-fortified Soviet bunker. After a five-day bombardment the Germans, under General Erich von Manstein, assaulted the Crimean port of Sebastopol on June 7, but were repulsed by fanatical defenders commanded by General Ivan E. Petrov. German firepower eventually prevailed, and on June 30 Petrov began an evacuation that was completed on July 3. The battle cost the Soviets some 150,000 troops, including 90,000 taken prisoner, with another 240,000 lost in battles on the adjacent Kerch Peninsula. Of the 30,000 civilians left in the fortress city, two-thirds were executed outright or deported to concentration camps.

Right: On June 28, *Fall Blau* got underway and made rapid advances. That was despite the fact that the sheer vastness of the Russian front overwhelmed Germany's belatedly expanding industrial capability to produce modern mechanized fighting and transport vehicles. In consequence, the horse returned as a valuable military asset, supplementing trucks in keeping the Germans supplied as they pushed inexorably eastward.

Left: Members of a French *"Freiwilliger"* (volunteer) unit pose for the Propaganda Ministry cameraman. The German invasion of the Soviet Union was accompanied by a general appeal within all the occupied countries for volunteers to join in Hitler's "anti-Bolshevik crusade." This raised units such as the Norwegian and Danish Fifth SS Panzer Division *"Wiking,"* as well as units made up of French, Dutch, Belgian Flemings, Walloons, and even anti-Stalinist Russians and Cossacks. Also fighting in Russia was the Spanish volunteer Blue Division, as well as Germany's formal allies, the Italians, Romanians, Hungarians, Slovaks, Croats, and the cobelligerent Finnish army.

Above: A German MG 34 machine-gun team scans the area
ahead as it covers an infantry assault on the Russian steppes.
After having lost 1.2 million men in their poorly conducted
counteroffensives throughout the winter and spring, Soviet
forces did not put up much resistance to the new German
offensive, leading Hitler to believe that the Red Army was
down to its last reserves and on the verge of collapse.
Germans advancing on the front may have taken note that
this time the Russians were withdrawing in good order.

Right: German mounted infantry revive another old use of the
horse, which became particularly widespread in the war behind
the lines against Soviet partisans. Many of the partisans were
Ukrainian Cossacks, and a good many other Cossacks, who
harbored a greater hatred of Stalin than of Hitler, rode for the
Germans. Germany's Romanian, Hungarian, Slovak, and
Croatian allies often served stints of duty fighting the partisans
as well. Given the guerrilla nature of these operations, atrocities
and reprisals on both sides became commonplace with quarter
neither offered nor expected.

Above: *Panzergrenadiers* advance on or alongside a Panzer III, now upgraded with a high-velocity 50mm cannon. On July 5, the Fourth Panzer Army began advancing toward the Don River and Voronezh. Pleased with Army Group South's progress, Hitler now divided it for a dual objective. Army Group A would proceed south to the Caucasus oil fields, while Army Group B would advance westward to secure the Volga River, particularly the city that bore the name of his primary enemy: Stalingrad.

Right: A US Marine private, holding a Garand M1 rifle with bayonet, poses with his sea bag laid out for inspection. Following the victory at Midway, the United States decided to take the offensive in the Pacific, choosing for its objective two islands that the Japanese had recently seized in the Solomon chain—Tulagi, where they were establishing a seaplane base, and a larger one on which they were building an airfield, called Guadalcanal. The Marines, who had already distinguished themselves in their valiant but hopeless defense of Wake Island on December 10–23, 1941, would make the initial assault.

Opposite page: The heavy cruiser *Quincy*, seen behind troopship *President Adams* at Noumea, New Caledonia, three days before the Guadalcanal landing, was surprised and sunk by a Japanese cruiser force commanded by Vice Admiral Gunichi Mikawa off Savo Island on the night of August 8, along with sister ships *Astoria* and *Vincennes*, and the Australian heavy cruiser *Canberra*. Fortunately for the Allies, Mikawa did not follow up on his victory, but it caused a shaken Vice Admiral Robert L. Ghormley to withdraw his fleet from the area on August 9. That in turn compelled Rear Admiral Frank Jack Fletcher to do the same with the transports he commanded—leaving the Marines on Guadalcanal to face the Japanese on their own.

Above: The first Allied offensive of World War II began with a virtually unopposed landing on August 7, as the Marines quickly secured the airfield, which they named Henderson Field. Although taken by surprise, the Japanese responded quickly. On August 8, the troop transport *President Jackson* and the Australian heavy cruiser *Australia*, both photographed from the destroyer *Ellet*, take evasive action as they come under attack from G4M1 bombers, escorted by Mitsubishi A6M2 Zero fighters from Rabaul.

Above: One of many G4Ms—soon to be codenamed "Betty" by the Allies— shot down in the failed attempt to destroy the Allied invasion force floats beside destroyer *Ellet* off Tulagi. The small island of Tulagi was secured by August 8, for the loss of 45 Marines and almost all of its 500-man garrison killed. The nearby islands of Gavutu and Tanambogo also fell quickly. The Japanese were determined to retake Guadalcanal, however, and soon began gathering land, naval, and air forces at Rabaul for that purpose.

Below: The destroyer *Buchanan*, shown refueling from the carrier *Wasp* while en route to Tulagi, typifies the "workhorses" of both the US and Japanese navies in the Solomons. *Wasp* was torpedoed and sunk, along with the destroyer *O'Brien*, by Japanese submarine *I-19* on September 15. In addition to regular escort and other duties, *Buchanan* had participated in the battles of Cape Esperance on October 11–12—during which one of her torpedoes helped sink Japanese heavy cruiser *Furutaka*— Guadalcanal on November 12, and Kolombangara on July 13, 1943.

Right: A wounded German who had lost his right arm is tended by medics—in what seems to be a training exercise staged for the camera. Such scenes became commonplace throughout the Eastern Front as casualties mounted, however—and especially frequent in Stalingrad as the defenders, despite galling losses of their own, kept up a stubborn resistance for every block and building.

Below: A German mortar team supports an infantry assault as *Fall Blau* presses onward in the face of stiffening Soviet resistance. Assaulted in August, the Black Sea port of Novorossiysk was abandoned by the Red Army on September 11, but a small naval contingent stubbornly held out in the district of Malaya Zemlya for the next 225 days. After taking Nalchik on October 28, Army Group A paused to secure a line between that city and Mozdok, where it would await resupply—and, with the fall of Stalingrad, reunification with Army Group B—in anticipation of resuming its advance into Azerbaijan the following spring.

Above: An American ammunition dump burns during the ongoing fight for Guadalcanal on November 26. Fighting malaria as well as a series of Japanese attacks, the Marines held onto Henderson Field, whose aircraft, combined with those of a returning Navy under Admiral William F. Halsey Jr., foiled one Japanese attempt after another to retake the island. After a wild series of naval night actions that climaxed with the American battleships *South Dakota* and *Washington* sinking the Japanese *Kirishima* on November 15, it no longer became a matter of whether the Marines, now joined by the US Army's 23rd "Americal" Division, would secure the island, but of when.

Above: German motorcycle dispatch riders take a break on the steppes before Stalingrad. Prior to the assault on the city, *Generaloberst* Wolfram von Richthofen's *Luftflotte* 4 bombed most of it into rubble, creating a firestorm on August 23. The male populace, however, either kept working in the ruins of their factories or fought in Workers Militias. The 16th Panzer Division reported having to trade "shot for shot" with the Soviet 1077th Anti-Aircraft Regiment until it knocked out or overran all 37 of its batteries—and was shocked to discover that the gunners had all been young women.

Right: A Russian woman, forced to live in the ruins of Stalingrad, cooks a meal amid the rubble of her former home, in the makeshift remnants of what had been a stove. Stalin is said to have refused to evacuate the city's civilians on the rationale that their continued presence would motivate the troops there to fight harder in its defense. As it was, thousands of reinforcements ferried into the city across the Volga under air and artillery attack were expended in costly counterattacks under threats from their commissars that anyone who balked would be shot.

Below: An exhausted platoon of *Panzergrenadiers* surveys its latest conquest on October 15—the Dzerzhinskiy Tractor Factory and adjacent houses in Stalingrad's northern district, which ten days earlier had been subjected to 900 dive-bombing sorties by Ju-87s of *Luftflotte* 4's *Sturzkampfgeschwader* (dive-bomber wings) 1, 2, and 77. With 90 percent of the city destroyed and their front reduced to a 3,000-foot (910m) section along the west bank of the Volga, General Vassily Chuikov's forces held on, supported by artillery firing from the east side of the river and a growing Soviet army air force.

Left: On September 30, with German forces stalled in Stalingrad, Hitler announced that they would never leave the city. *Reichsmarshall* Hermann Göring assured him that even if the Sixth Army was cut off, he would keep it supplied from the air. In practice, this did not happen; even with bombers and other less-suitable planes to supplement the transports, such as this Ju-52/3m bringing in medical supplies and evacuating wounded, the *Luftwaffe* was averaging 94 tons (85 tonnes) of matériel for a still-embattled army whose daily requirement was 117 tons (106 tonnes). Soviet anti-aircraft fire, fighter planes, the weather, and accidents accounted for a total of 488 of aircraft committed to Göring's failed "Air Bridge."

Right: Better clothed for the winter of 1942, Germans examine mail from the Fatherland. For the Sixth Army in Stalingrad, deliveries of mail—or anything else—soon became a rarity. On November 19, Marshal Zhukov and General Aleksandr M. Vassilievsky launched Operation Uranus, in which General Nikolai F. Vatutin smashed through the Romanian Third, Italian Eighth, and Hungarian Second armies along the Sixth Army's northern flank. The next day a Soviet offensive to the south bypassed the German Fourth Panzer Army and crushed the Romanian IV Corps. On November 22, the two Soviet forces met near Kalach. On December 12, Field Marshal Erich von Manstein let loose Operation Winter Storm, seeking to open a corridor to Stalingrad, but after initially being taken by surprise the Red Army slowed the German advance. On December 16 the Soviets launched Operation Little Saturn, intended to cut off German forces in the Caucasus, smashing the Italian Eighth Army in the process. On the 23rd, Manstein canceled his offensive, leaving the German Sixth Army completely encircled.

Right: A Lockheed Hudson Mark IV of the Middle East Communications Flight overflies the pyramids of Egypt, where the British intended to make their final stand. With General Claude Auckinleck taking personal charge from Ritchie, the Eighth Army managed to halt Rommels's advance around El Alamein during July 1942, but his counterattacks failed. In August Churchill replaced Auckinleck as Commander-in-Chief, Middle East, with General Sir Harold Alexander and placed Lieutenant General Bernard Law Montgomery in charge of the Eighth Army.

Left: An *Africa Korps* machine gun team takes up a defensive position, pending Rommels's next move. A German assault at Alam el Halfa Ridge on August 30 failed, after which Montgomery meticulously rebuilt his forces and planned his counterstroke, which relied on the elimination of thousands of Axis-laid mines. The Second Battle of El Alamein finally began on October 23 and by November 4 Rommel, his line crumbling, was begging Hitler's permission to withdraw. Hitler never replied, and on November 5 Rommel, on his own initiative, began a 500-mile (800km) retreat. He had lost 75,000 troops, 1,000 guns, and 500 tanks, along with any hope of taking Egypt.

Above: The US Navy escort carrier *Santee* lies off the coast of Morocco with a deckload of Douglas SBD-3 Dauntless dive bombers and Grumman F4F-4 Wildcats to support Operation Torch, the Anglo-American invasion of Vichy French Morocco and Algeria on November 8, 1942. French opposition was overcome in a matter of days, placing the US Army in position to threaten Axis forces in Tunisia from the west while Montgomery closed in from the east.

Left: Americans present a squadron of Curtiss P-40s to Free French forces in Algiers. In the wake of Operation Torch, the Germans occupied southern France on November 11, which among other consequences saw the scuttling of the French fleet in Toulon before they could seize it and an en-masse defection of soldiers outside the country back into the Allied camp. More than two years after they sentenced Charles de Gaulle to death as a traitor, the only Frenchmen left administering the country under German rule, such as Marshal Pétain and Pierre Laval, now themselves stood to face treason charges if the Allies won the war.

Chapter 5

On to the Offensive

Opposite page: First Lieutenant William C. Lawrence peers down from his bombardier's position in the nose of a Consolidated B-24H Liberator of the Eighth Air Force's Second Bomb Division. His American-developed Norden bombsight, much touted for its accuracy, was covered with a bag before the photograph was taken. For a time, the Second Bomb Division's operations officer was Hollywood star James Stewart, who flew 24 combat missions over a variety of targets, including Berlin.

By 1942, the tide of war had begun to turn. At Midway in June, and at Second Alamein, Guadalcanal, and Stalingrad in November, the initiative had been wrested from the Axis. The question in 1943 was whether the Allies would seize that initiative or the Axis would recover it.

Several pivotal events occurred in July 1943. In the Solomon Islands, the Americans landed on New Georgia, precipitating another round of land, air, and sea battles that resulted in further attrition to Japan's ships, planes, and best-trained sailors and airmen. In Russia, a German attack on the Soviet salient around Kursk climaxed in the largest tank battle in history—and ended with Soviet forces henceforth on the offensive. At the same time, the Americans and British landed on Sicily, causing a crisis in Rome that led to the downfall of Benito Mussolini and forced the Germans to draw precious resources from the Eastern Front to shore up their southern defenses—especially after Italy's government capitulated on September 8.

The end of the year saw the Allies almost universally on the march, with the Soviets driving the Germans from the eastern Ukraine, a number of Allied armies slogging their way up the Italian boot, the US Marines at the top of the Solomons on Bougainville, the nearby Japanese base of Rabaul effectively neutralized, and the first American landings in the Central Pacific taking place in the Gilbert Islands, including bloody Tarawa. Only in Asia did the Axis remain a threat, as the Japanese army still strove to push into China and even into India.

Left: President Franklin D. Roosevelt and Prime Minister Winston Churchill head a gathering of military officers at the Casablanca Conference, held between January 14 and 24, 1943. Among its resolutions was a call for the unconditional surrender of the Axis powers, joint leadership of Free French forces to be shared by Generals Charles de Gaulle and Henri Giraud, aid to the Soviet Union, and the invasion of occupied Europe through Sicily and Italy. To the disappointment of Josef Stalin, who did not attend the conference because he was overseeing the Battle of Stalingrad, the Allies decided against staging an "across channel invasion" of German-occupied France in 1943.

Above: A German artillery observer reports Soviet activity and points out targets to his gunners during the winter of 1943. On January 30, as Soviet forces closed in on Stalingrad, General Friedrich Paulus was promoted to field marshal by Adolf Hitler, in tacit expectation that he and his surrounded Sixth Army would win or die. The next day, even to the surprise of his captors, Paulus surrendered. By February 2, the Battle of Stalingrad was over, having cost the Russians 1,129,619 casualties and the Axis 841,000, including 91,000 prisoners—only 5,000 of whom would return to Germany in 1955. Meanwhile, facing the prospect of being cut off, German Army Group A began withdrawing from the Caucasus. Resurgent Soviet forces saw the last Germans out of the region on February 4. The failure of Hitler's ambitious *Fall Blau* was complete.

Above: One of seven Japanese transports out of an 11-ship convoy sunk or disabled by American planes on November 15, 1942, *Kinugawa Maru* was run ashore in order to get its troops onto Guadalcanal. This was a monument to the spirit that earned Rear Admiral Raizo Tanaka the American nickname "Tenacious Tanaka," and his regular convoys the sobriquet of "Tokyo Express." By 1943, however, the brilliant but outspoken Tanaka had been transferred to Singapore and his successor, Rear Admiral Tomiji Koyonagi, was engaged in evacuating, not reinforcing, the island. On February 8, the last of 11,000 surviving Japanese were removed; the next day, the Americal Division's commander, Major General Alexander M. Patch, radioed Admiral Halsey, "Tokyo Express no longer has terminus on Guadalcanal." Also in American hands was the initiative in the Pacific.

Above: *Marder* III antitank vehicles—PAK 40 75mm guns mounted on the modified chassis of captured Czechoslovakian Type 38 light tanks— roll through a Ukrainian village. Although Soviet forces followed up their Stalingrad victory to retake Kharkov, Belgorod, and Kursk in early February 1943, they became overextended, and on February 19 Field Marshal Erich von Manstein launched a brilliant counterattack that by March 6 had destroyed or depleted four Soviet armies and inflicted more than 81,000 casualties. The Germans secured Kharkov on March 16 and recovered Belgorod on March 18. The initiative in the East was once more up for grabs.

Right: Members of the 16/5th Lancers clean the 6-pounder cannon barrel of their Crusader Mark III tank at El Aroussa before joining the drive on Tunis. On March 6, an ailing Rommel struck at the British Eighth Army at Medenine, only to lose some 40 tanks. Montgomery summed things up in a letter to Sir Alan Brooke that day: "He is trying to attack me in daylight with tanks, followed by lorried infantry . . . It is an absolute gift, and the man must be mad." On March 10, Rommel returned to Germany to appeal to Hitler to evacuate Axis forces from a now-hopeless position. Hitler refused, choosing instead to send more reinforcements to Tunisia.

Above: In response to superlative Soviet armor such as the T-34 medium and Klimenti Voroshilov KV-1 heavy tank, the Germans developed the 57-ton (51.7 tonne) *Panzerkampfwagen* Mark VI Tiger. Boasting armor as thick as 4.7 inches (11.9cm) and armed with the deadly 88mm gun, the Tiger tank made a daunting impression on Allied tankers, but, fortunately for them, only 1,347 were built between August 1942 and August 1944. Some were parceled out to the German Tenth Panzer Division in Tunisia. There, on February 19, 1943, Field Marshal Erwin Rommel struck back at the Allies at Kasserine Pass, inflicting 10,000 casualties—most of them American—and destroying 183 tanks and 706 trucks for the loss of 2,000 men and 34 tanks by February 25. At that point, however, he pulled back.

Left: An embarrassing performance by the Americans at Kasserine Pass led to a critical reappraisal of US Army operational and training doctrine. It also led to the replacement of the II Corps commander, Major General Lloyd Fredendall, with Major General George S. Patton Jr. on March 6. As Patton resumed the advance into south-central Tunisia, on March 23, *Generalleutnant* Friedrich *Freiherr* von Broich attacked with the Tenth Panzer Division at El Guettar, but he ran afoul of mine fields and a surprisingly spirited American defense that cost him 30 of his 50 tanks. Patton retook the offensive and ultimately handed the United States its first land victory in North Africa—and its first glimpse of his formidable tactical talents.

Left: Italian prisoners taken during Patton's follow-up to El Guettar play cards within a barbed wire enclosure on April 1. Although Patton was disappointed not to have matched wits with Rommel, he came up against Italy's best general, Giovanni Messe, whose troops conducted a stout defense of Hill 369 between March 30 and April 3; Messe's troops defended Hill 772 thereafter, with backing by the 21st Panzer Division. Finally, in the face of overwhelming Allied forces on both fronts, Messe evacuated the remainder of Hill 772's defenders on the night of April 6.

Right: British crewmen set up a 40mm Bofors anti-aircraft gun in preparation for an enemy air attack on the Goubillat Plain near Medjaz-el-Bab, during their final advance on Tunis. After a month of fighting, Tunis fell to the British on May 7, and on May 13 *Generaloberst* Jürgen von Arnim surrendered the last of his forces. Benito Mussolini's African empire was no more and, in a Stalingrad-like ending, the 230,000 Italian and German soldiers that Hitler refused to evacuate from Tunisia became prisoners. The Allies now prepared for their next objectives: Sardinia, Sicily, and, from there, the Italian mainland.

Below: A crewman on a 110-foot (33.5m) US Navy sub chaser scans the sky for enemy patrol planes and the sea for U-boats in April 1943. The Battle of the Atlantic reached its climax between March and May 1943, when U-boat wolf packs initially came close to sinking more cargo ships than could sustain Britain but ended with the escorts inflicting such heavy losses that German Admiral Karl Dönitz temporarily recalled his undersea raiders. From then on, the Allies slowly gained the upper hand in the critical struggle for control of the North Atlantic seaways.

Opposite page: A Consolidated PB4Y-1 Liberator bomber departs on an antisubmarine patrol over the Bay of Biscay in the summer of 1943. For all the valiant efforts of the small warships and escort carrier-backed Hunter-Killer groups, the greatest nemesis of German U-boats was the gauntlet they had to run in and out of their French bases. Within that relatively small area, they had no choice, when spotted by a Liberator, Sunderland flying boat, or other maritime patrol plane but to either submerge to a relatively low depth or duel it out using an increasingly heavy arsenal of antiaircraft guns. By the end of the war, 30,000 out of 40,000 German submariners had lost their lives.

Above: A U-boat heads out to join a wolf pack in the North Atlantic in the spring of 1943. After an embarrassingly unproductive performance by heavy cruiser *Admiral Hipper* and *Panzerschiff Lützow* against a gallantly defended British convoy in the Barents Sea on December 31, 1942, Hitler threatened to scrap his entire High Seas Fleet and accepted the resignation of Grand Admiral Erich Raeder. Karl Dönitz took over command of the *Kriegsmarine* and put its emphasis on an all-out submarine campaign against Allied convoys.

Right: A crash-landed Mitsubishi A6M3 Zero lies abandoned on Munda, New Georgia. When introduced in August 1940, the A6M2 Zero had been the finest carrier-based fighter in the world, but by 1943 a new generation of American fighters was surpassing it and taking a growing toll on the irreplaceable trained and experienced Zero pilots over the Solomons. Between April 1 and 13, Japanese Admiral Isoroku Yamamoto launched an air offensive, Operation I-Go, which caused considerable damage but failed to stem the Allied advance. On April 18, as Yamamoto was flying to inspect units on Ballale—news of which American radios had intercepted and decoded—his G4M1 bomber-transport and its Zero escorts were ambushed by P-38Gs of the 339th Fighter Squadron, and Japan's ablest admiral-in-chief was killed in action near Bougainville.

Above: Two damaged US Marine Vought F4U-1A Corsairs await repair or salvage on Torokina airfield, Bougainville. Rejected by the Navy as unsuitable for carrier operations, the Corsair was passed on to the Marines on Henderson Field, Guadalcanal, whose fighter squadron VMF-124 first flew them in combat on February 14, 1943. After a shaky start, by May the Marines had learned to play the F4U's strengths —a speed of more than 400mph (640kph) and the punch of six wing-mounted .50-caliber machine guns—to get the measure of Japan's more maneuverable but slower and flimsier A6M3 Zero.

Right: Members of Marine torpedo bomber squadron VMTB-232 pose before their unit's mission scoreboard. Operating Douglas SBD Dauntless dive bombers from Henderson Field, scout bombing VMSB-232 was the first such unit to go into action during the Guadalcanal campaign, serving there from August 20 through October 12, 1942. Reequipped with Gurmman TBF-1s and redesignated VMTB-232, the squadron resumed operations from Espiritu Santo in July 1943, moving up to newly recurred Munda airfield on New Georgia to support the Allied advance toward Bougainville and strike at the Japanese base at Rabaul.

Right: Seen here in an incongruously pastoral setting, RAF Wing Commander Guy Gibson flew Avro Manchester and Lancaster bombers as well as Bristol Beaufighters, in which he shot down four German airplanes at night. Later, on the night of May 16, 1943, he led modified Lancasters of No. 617 Squadron as they dropped cylindrical "bouncing bombs" specially designed by Barnes Wallis to breech the Mohne and Eder dams. The success of Operation Chastise in flooding the Ruhr industrial district, combined with his previous outstanding leadership, earned Gibson the Victoria Cross. Insisting on returning to combat despite having already flown 174 combat missions, Gibson was killed near Steenbergen, Netherlands, while flying a deHavilland Mosquito Mark XX on a pathfinder mission on the night of September 19, 1944.

Above: US Navy personnel man a .50-caliber machine gun by the Amchitka waterfront in 1943. On June 3, 1942, Japanese carriers *Ryujo* and *Junyo* raided Dutch Harbor, Alaska, in a diversion meant to lead the Americans to divide their fleet assets before the Battle of Midway. Additionally, the Japanese occupied Attu and Kiska in the Aleutian Islands, starting a campaign in what Americans called the "Birthplace of Bad Weather" that became a misery for both sides.

Right: A US Navy pilot attached to a Consolidated PBY-5A Catalina squadron in Alaska checks the operations board on March 7, 1943. On May 11, 1943, the Americans landed on Attu, where Colonel Yasuyo Yamasaki subjected them to a grueling campaign that cost them 3,929 casualties until May 29, when Yamasaki led a suicidal charge at Massacre Bay and died alongside 2,351 of his remaining men. On August 15, 34,426 Allied troops, of whom 5,300 were Canadian, landed on Kiska, only to discover that a Japanese task force had already slipped through to evacuate the entire garrison on July 28.

Below: New *Panzerkampfwagen* Mark V Panther medium tanks maneuver before deployment in the Battle of Kursk. Although armed with high-velocity 75mm L70 cannons and superior armor to the T-34, the Panther was too heavy for its engine and suspension, and early models often caught fire in the field. On July 4, 1943, 435,000 Germans, with 3,156 tanks, struck at the Kursk salient from north and south, only to grind to a halt against belts of Soviet antitank defenses, behind which waited 1,087,500 Soviet troops and 3,375 tanks. A final, eight-hour armored clash at Prokhorovka on July 12 ended in a costly stalemate for both sides.

Right: Junkers Ju-87D Stukas sally forth to engage Soviet strongpoints or armor. In addition to being the largest tank battle in history, Kursk saw an equally epic low-level air battle between 2,110 German and 2,792 Soviet aircraft. The Soviets admitted losing 1,627 planes, but the 681 the Germans lost were irreplaceable. On July 17, the Soviets launched their own offensives north and south of the salient to retake Oryol and Belgorod on August 5, and secure Kharkov on August 23. They had decisively thwarted the blitzkrieg and would remain on the offensive for the rest of the war.

Below: Megaphone in hand, the boat captain aboard the US Navy attack transport *Leonard Wood* (APA-12) watches as Higgins LCM(3) landing craft, mechanized head for Sicily's beaches on July 10, 1943. Operation Husky began with a costly airborne invasion, followed by an amphibious landing. On July 19, Rome suffered its first bombing attack. On July 25 Mussolini was replaced as Prime Minister by Marshal Pietro Badoglio and arrested, compelling Hitler to divert forces from Russia to avert a potential collapse in Italy. While Montgomery's Eighth Army fought its way up Sicily's east coast, Lieutenant General George Patton's Seventh Army made a swift end run through the west, but an incident in which Patton berated and slapped two soldiers suffering from combat fatigue led to his temporary removal. On August 17, the last 60,000 Germans and 75,000 Italians were evacuated from Sicily across the Straits of Messina.

Above: A British heavy artillery piece pounds a German position in Italy. On September 3, American, British, Canadian, and Indian troops landed on the Italian mainland, at Salerno, Calabria, and Taranto. On September 8, the Italian government capitulated and agreed to become a cobelligerent of the Allies. While German units seized control in Rome and elsewhere in northern and central Italy, their Tenth Army under *Generaloberst* Heinrich von Vietinghoff tried to destroy or at least contain the Allied beachhead until September 18, when it began pulling back.

Left: On September 12, after being shown all over Italy, Mussolini was being held at Campo Imperator on Gran Sasso in the Appenine Mountains. On that day, German airborne troops, led by Austrian-born commando *SS-Sturmbahnführer* Otto Skorzeny, landed by glider, overwhelmed the Italian guards without a shot being fired, freed *Il Duce*, and, using the Fieseler Fi.156 *Storch* shown, flew him off the mountain and on to Vienna. Hitler installed Mussolini as the figurehead of the *Repubblica Sociale Italiana*, or RSI, which kept northern Italy fighting on the Axis side.

Left: Cobelligerent Italian soldiers familiarize Sergeant P. Hopkinson, a member of the Royal Engineers attached to their unit, how to use the sight on their artillery piece. In the wake of Italy's capitulation, part of its armed forces and equipment went to the Allies, but much was seized by the Germans, who, under the leadership of Field Marshal Albert Kesselring, began fortifying Italy's rivers and mountains with a series of defensive lines. What Winston Churchill wishfully called the "soft underbelly of Europe" proved to be, in the words of one British soldier, a "tough old gut."

Left: Two members of the US Eighth Air Force relax between missions in the 381st Bombardment Group's officer's club at Ridgewell, Essex, with a record of missions already flown emblazoned on the wall. One of the group's worst ordeals occurred on August 17, 1943, when it participated in the raid on German ball bearing factories at Schweinfurt, in concert with another on the Messerschmitt factory at Regensburg. With a total of 60 bombers and five fighters the Eighth Air Force destroyed—against 40 German fighter losses—the 381st lost the most of any group that day: 9 of the 20 B-17s it sent.

Above: Master Sergeant Bingham watches Sergeant Pilla add to the mission tally of Idiot's Delight, a B-17F of the 332nd Squadron, 94th Bomb Group. On October 14, the Eighth Air Force attacked Schweinfurt again, halting ball bearing production for another one and a half months, but it did so at a cost of 59 bombers that were shot down, one ditched in the Channel, five crashed, and 12 scrapped due to battle damage. The Americans claimed 186 enemy fighters, but the Luftwaffe only recorded 38 lost. That attrition rate suspended operations for a time and put the sustainability of the entire daylight bombing campaign in question.

Left: Focke-Wulf Fw-190As modified for ground attack duties line up for a propaganda photo before being painted in yellow Eastern Front recognition bands and sent to Russia. First entering combat in the fall of 1941, the Fw-190 proved a match for the latest Allied fighters and also capable of carrying a variety of weaponry. Specialized Fw-190F and Fw-190G ground attack planes attached to *Schlachtgeschwader* (battle wings) took a heavy toll on Soviet equipment, while cannon-armed Fw-190A-8s attached to *Sturmgruppen* (storm groups) charged head-on into American bomber formations, often with devastating results.

Above: After initial problems with their torpedoes, US Navy submarines became increasingly effective against Japanese merchant vessels and even warships. In August 1943, Lieutenant Commander Edward Steichen photographed an exercise aboard the newly commissioned *Gato*-class sub *Cero* off Groton, Connecticut, in which its captain, Commander David C. White, sights through the periscope and Lieutenant Commander David H. McClintock watches crewmen at the control dials.

Above: A Grumman F6F-3 Hellcat of Navy fighter squadron VF-33 burns after crashing at Ondonga on December 10, 1943. Just north of New Georgia, Ondonga's 4,500-by-200-foot (1,371-by-91m) airfield was completed by the 37th and 82nd Construction Battalions in a record 25 days, on October 23. The first unit to fly the new F6F in combat, VF-33 started operations from Henderson Field on August 30, moved up to Segi Point, New Georgia, on October 19, and moved to Ondonga on November 30. It was credited with a total of 76.5 enemy planes during its Solomons tour, for the loss of ten pilots.

Right: Admiral Chester W. Nimitz, commander-in-chief, Pacific (CINCPAC), confers with two officers aboard a transport in Pearl Harbor in October 1943. On August 31, Nimitz opened a new series of offensive operations in the Central Pacific when three of his new-generation carriers, *Essex, Yorktown* and *Independence*, raided Marcus Island. This was followed by strikes at Tarawa and Makin on September 18 and 19, and Wake on October 5 and 6.

Below: Edward Steichen photographed Lieutenant Commander Paul D. Buie, commander of VF-16, briefing his pilots aboard the second *Lexington* (CV-16). During the Wake raid on October 5, Ensign Robert Duncan of *Yorktown's* VF-5 claimed the carrier-based Hellcat victory over a Zero (although land-based VF-33 had already met and mastered them over the Solomons in September). Buie downed one for his first of nine victories, and his squadron accounted for another three. The Hellcat units claimed a total of 27 victories without loss; the Japanese on Wake recorded 15 Zeros and pilots lost out of the 23 they had sent up, with another three pilots returning wounded.

Left: Marines man a 75mm pack howitzer on newly seized Torokina field on Bougainville Island. The Marines landed at this northern rung of the Solomons ladder on November 1, and that night a naval light cruiser and destroyer force commanded by Rear Admiral Aaron S. "Tip" Merrill managed to repulse a Japanese task force that had come to bombard the beachhead in the Battle of Empress Augusta Bay, sinking the light cruiser *Sendai* and destroyer *Hatsukaze* and damaging several other ships.

Right: After the victory at Empress Augusta Bay, a B-24 spotted seven Japanese cruisers and a dozen other ships heading for Rabaul. Lacking enough surface ships to counter this fresh threat to the Bougainville beachhead, Admiral William Halsey dispatched the two carriers at his disposal, *Saratoga*—shown here—and *Princeton*, with orders, as *Saratoga's* Lieutenant Commander Joseph J. Clifton recalled, "to cripple all of them that we could rather than concentrate on sinking a few." Raiding Rabaul's Simpson Harbor on November 5, the carriers succeeded in damaging all seven cruisers, forcing the Japanese to cancel their attack, for the loss of 13 of their 97 participating aircraft.

Left: Looking aft, F6F-3 Hellcats, Eastern Aircraft-built TBM-1 Avengers and SBD-5 Dauntlesses warm up their engines for a mission. On November 11, *Yorktown's* sister ships *Essex* and *Bunker Hill*, and light carrier *Independence*, joined *Saratoga* and *Princeton* for a follow-up raid on Rabaul that caused more damage but also drew an all-out counterstrike. The defending Hellcat squadrons claimed a grossly exaggerated 137 victories, but they did successfully defend the carriers. In the process, they not only annihilated Rabaul's air strength but rendered the once-formidable base impotent, to be bypassed rather than taken in the next Allied advance.

Above: Steichen caught one of *Lexington's* flight deck crewmen making the most of a brief lull in softening-up operations in preparation for the November 20 invasions of Makin and Tarawa in the Gilbert Islands. The US Army's 27th Infantry Division secured Makin on November 23 with only 66 dead and 185 wounded, compared to 395 Japanese killed and 3 captured, along with 101 Korean laborers. The Navy, however, suffered 697 dead, including 43 in a turret fire aboard battleship *Mississippi* on November 20, and 644 when escort carrier *Liscombe Bay* was sunk by Japanese submarine I-175 on November 24.

Left: Steichen photographed two SBD-5s being spotted for takeoff on *Lexington*'s after deck during the Gilberts operation. In contrast to Makin, the well-prepared bunkers and pillboxes on Tarawa atoll's main island of Betio stood up to a devastating bombardment, and, during the landing on November 20, most landing craft could not clear the surrounding reef, forcing the Marines to wade a quarter mile to the beach under withering fire. In consequence, it cost the lives of 990 Marines and 687 naval personnel to secure Betio on November 23, after killing 4,713 defenders and taking only 17 Japanese and 129 Koreans prisoner.

Below: Another Steichen photo shows an F6F returning to *Lexington* while deck crewmen look on from an SBD's wing and a TBF, wings folded, taxis to a forward parking area. After the Gilberts operation, *Lexington* raided Kawajalein in the Marshalls on December 4, sinking cargo ship *Kembu Maru* and damaging two cruisers while its pilots claimed 30 victories. At 23:32 hours that night, however, a nocturnally operating G4M landed a starboard torpedo hit that jammed the carrier's steering gear and killed nine men. After repairs in Bremerton, Washington, *Lexington* rejoined Task Force 58 as Vice Admiral Marc A. Mitscher's flagship on March 8, 1944.

Right: Marines wounded during the fighting on Bougainville are unloaded from a Douglas R4D transport at Vella la Vella for hospitalization. Between November 6 and 19, the Third Marine and 37th Infantry divisions began expanding the beachhead beyond Torokina. It took the Marines from December 9 to 27 to eliminate artillery batteries along a 300-foot (91m) ridge overlooking the Torokina River that they called "Hellzapoppin Ridge." Malaria and other tropical diseases caused as many casualties as the enemy. Australian, New Zealand, and Fijian troops continued the slow advance in 1944, but the last holdouts north and south of the island did not surrender before Japan itself had.

Below: Tech Sergeant Arthur J. Benko poses atop his B-24D *The Goon* of the 374th Squadron, 308th Bomb Group, attached to Major General Claire L. Chennault's Fourteenth Air Force in China, while Major Robert F. Bennett examines its mission tally. Benko was credited with 18 Japanese fighters, including 7 during a raid on Haiphong on October 1, 1943. In an attack on the Kowloon Docks early in December, two of *The Goon*'s engines were disabled and First Lieutenant Samuel J. Skousen ordered the crew to bail out. With the plane thus lightened, Skousen brought it back to base, and all of the crew returned except two—Benko and the bombardier, Second Lieutenant Malcolm S. Sanders, whom the Japanese captured and subsequently crucified. The repaired *Goon* kept operating until shot down on February 1, 1945.

Chapter 6

The Hard Road Back

Opposite page: American troops advance cautiously through the jungles beyond Hollandia in April 1944. On April 22, the 24th and 41st Infantry divisions, supported by the Fifth Fleet, landed in Tanahmerah and Humboldt bays to overrun Hollandia, while the 41st Division's 163rd Infantry Regiment landed at Aitape. In a highly successful example of General Douglas MacArthur's strategy of hopping from one strategically significant objective to the next along the northern New Guinea coast, both locations and their four airfields had been secured by April 27, isolating the Japanese Eighteenth Army at Wewak and virtually annihilating the Japanese Fourth Air Army.

The year 1944 began with encouraging signs for the Allies. On January 27, Soviet forces broke the siege of Leningrad, and on February 17 Marshals Ivan Konev and Nikolai Vatutin encircled and eliminated 56,000 German troops in the Korsun-Chekassy pocket. On January 28, however, Vatutin was ambushed by anti-Stalinist Ukrainian insurgents. He died of his wounds on April 14.

Moving from the Gilberts to the Marshall Islands, the Americans took Kawajalein on February 3, 1944, and Eniwetok on February 23. The Fifth Fleet also devastated the Japanese naval base at Truk in the Carolines on February 17 and supported landings at Hollandia, New Guinea, on April 22.

On February 20, the American and British air forces in Britain and Italy launched a continuous succession of escorted bombing missions against Axis cities, the primary mission of which was to draw the *Luftwaffe* into a decisive air battle. By the time "Big Week," as the Allies called the six-day air onslaught, ended on February 25, Allied fighters, including new North American P-51B Mustangs, had destroyed 355 German fighters and killed 100 pilots. It was the beginning of the end of German air superiority even over the Reich itself.

In Italy, the Allied drive to Rome was frustrated at Monte Cassino from January 17 through May 18. An Allied force also slipped 55 miles (88km) up the west coast to land at Anzio and Nettuno on January 22, but an overly cautious follow-up and a swift German reaction put the beachhead under siege until May 25.

Right: A Japanese pillbox and adjacent building show the effects of bombardment by Admiral Raymond C. Spruance's Fifth Fleet and by aircraft of Vice Admiral Marc A. Mitscher's Task Force 58 in preparation for the landings on January 31, 1944. The Japanese defense in the Marshalls relied heavily on six airfields, but the Americans eliminated them. Unlike at Tarawa, however, even after devastating Kwajalein with the "Spruance Haircut" and "Mitscher Shampoo," the carrier planes gave the troops constant close support until the atoll was secured on February 3. The result: 7,870 Japanese killed and 105 captured, compared to 372 American dead and 1,592 wounded.

Below: Begrimed and weary from two days and nights of fighting on Eniwetok Atoll, a member of the 22nd Marine Regiment takes time out for coffee. Engebi Island fell in six hours on February 18, but the 106th Infantry Regiment encountered stiffer-than-expected resistance on Eniwetok Island, requiring February 19 to 21 to secure it. Parry Island took 900 tons (816 tonnes) of battleship shelling before the 22nd Marines landed there on February 22. The entire atoll was secured on February 23, with 2,677 Japanese dead at a cost of 262 Americans killed and 77 missing.

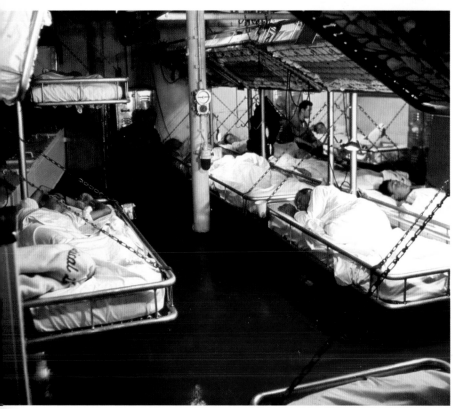

Above: A view of the carrier Yorktown's sick bay early in its cruise with Task Force 58. To support the Eniwetok landings, on February 17, TF 58 struck at Japan's main Central Pacific naval base, Truk Atoll. By the time the Americans withdrew on February 18, they had sunk two light cruisers, four destroyers, and 40 other ships and destroyed 270 aircraft, for the loss of 25 planes and a damaging torpedo hit to the carrier Intrepid. When 100 more aircraft gathered at Truk, TF 58 raided it again on April 29–30 and then bypassed it in the Allied advance.

Right: A control Jeep manned by Captains Larry Roth and Wallace E. Marquardt directs a B-24J of the Eighth Air Force to the runway of a British airfield for takeoff. Although not as rugged as the B-17, the B-24 could carry more bombs—5,000 pounds (2,268kg) compared to a B-17G's 4,500 (2,041kg) on a long-range mission—and was the most-produced bomber of the war, with a total of 18,482 being built.

Left: Captain Louis Detoni adjusts his oxygen mask in preparation for a mission with the Eighth Air Force in 1944. In January, Major General James H. Doolittle, who had previously held command of the Fifteenth Air Force from its inception in Italy on November 1, 1943, as the strategic bombing arm to operate over southern and eastern Europe, arrived to take charge of the "Mighty Eighth." On March 13, he became the first Army Reserve officer to be promoted to Lieutenant General.

Above: Ground crewmen of VIII Fighter Command display typical payloads that a North American P-51 Mustang might carry on a given sortie, including .50-caliber machine gun rounds, 500-pound (226kg) bombs for tactical missions and long-range underwing tanks for escorting the bombers. The first American unit in England to receive the P-51B, the 354th Fighter Group of the Ninth Air Force, flew its first mission from Boxted on December 1, 1943, accompanied by Lieutenant Colonel Donald Blakeslee of the Eighth Air Force's Fourth Fighter Group, who immediately declared that he wanted Mustangs in place of his group's P-47 Thunderbolts.

Above: A P-51B of the 355th Fighter Group practices flying in formation among B-17Gs of the 381st Bomb Group. The first Eighth Air Force group fully equipped with P-51s, the 357th, flew its first mission on February 11, 1944, and the Fourth Fighter Group, reequipped per Don Blakeslee's fervent wishes, flew its first Mustang mission on February 28. As the agile long-ranged P-51 proved its worth, more units were reequipped until, by the end of the war, the P-47-equipped 56th Fighter Group was the only one in the Eighth Air Force not flying the Mustang.

Left: An English woman engaged in farm work harvests oats beside an Eighth Air Force airfield in 1944. On March 4, 502 B-17s attacked industrial targets in the suburbs of Berlin, but bad weather forced many to strike at other targets of opportunity. Losses came to 15 B-17s, four P-47s, four P-38s, and no less than 16 P-51s. Two days later, 700 bombers struck at "Big B" again in the face of everything the *Luftwaffe* could throw up against them, losing 53 B-17s, 16 B-24s, five P-51s, five P-47s, and one P-38, while the fighters claimed 82 German planes in return.

Left: Pilots of No. 453 Squadron, Royal Australian Air Force, are briefed at Ford Airfield in May 1944. Originally equipped with Brewster Buffaloes, 453 Squadron was badly mauled at the hands of the Japanese army air force during the Malayan campaign in 1941–42. Reconstituted, it resumed operations from Drem, Scotland, and, equipped with the Supermarine Spitfire Mark IX, it escorted bombers or carried out its own offensive sweeps over France.

Below: First arriving in Burma in March 1942, Lieutenant General William Slim rose amid the British debacle there to command the Fourteenth Army. Under his leadership, as well as the training of Major General Orde Wingate—until his tragic death in a plane crash on March 24, 1944—British Commonwealth troops learned to fight in the Southeast Asian jungles and beat the Japanese at their own game. After foiling Japanese attempts to invade India in the battles of the Admin Box (February 4–23, 1944), Imphal (March 8–July 3), and Kohima (April 4–June 22), Slim's troops prepared to carry their own offensive into Burma.

Right: Lord Louis Mountbatten addresses the crew of a US Navy ship. With a distinguished combat career in the Royal Navy behind him, Mountbatten was appointed Supreme Allied Commander, Southeast Asia Command, in October 1943. As was the case with General Dwight D. Eisenhower in Europe, Mountbatten and his chief of staff, US Army Major General Albert C. Wedemeyer, not only had to deal with the Japanese threat to India, but also had to diplomatically balance such clashing personalities as General William Slim, General Joseph W. Stilwell, Major General Claire L. Chennault, and *Generalissimo* Chiang Kai-shek.

Left: North American B-25J Mitchell bombers of the Twelfth Air Force fly in support of Lieutenant General Mark W. Clark's Fifth Army in Italy. On January 16, Allied forces tried to breach the German Gustav Line through the Liri Valley by assaulting Monte Cassino, only to be repulsed. Convinced that German troops were occupying the 14th-century monastery on top of the mountain, the Allies demolished it on February 15 with 1,400 tons (1,270 tonnes) of bombs. The result was a propaganda coup for the Germans, who, on orders from Field Marshal Albert Kesselring, had never been in the monastery and used the rubble as additional cover to frustrate further Allied assaults.

Right: DUKW (a US Army designation for a 1942-designed utility vehicle with all-wheel drive and two powered rear axles) amphibious trucks transport cargo across Anzio Beach. On January 22, American and British forces moved 55 miles (88km) up the Italian west coast to land at Anzio and Nettuno, taking the Germans by surprise and unwittingly placing themselves in position to forge ahead and take Rome. American VI Corps commander Lieutenant General John P. Lucas spent too much time consolidating his beachhead, however, and, by January 29, when he had 69,000 troops ashore, the Germans had rushed in 71,500 to contain the threat.

Left: German prisoners, most apparently *Luftwaffe* personnel, are issued C rations at a US Army prisoner holding center at Anzio. The Allies finally attacked on January 30, but the British First Division got no farther than Camplolone, forming a vulnerable salient, and the American Third Division was stopped at Cisterna. On February 4, the Germans counterattacked, pushing the Allies back to a desperately held "final beachhead line" before both sides were too exhausted to continue. The Germans attacked again on February 29 but were stopped with 2,500 casualties.

Below: DUKWs and soldiers pass by a German pillbox, damaged buildings, and debris in Anzio as the Allies fight to survive on their still-tenuous beachhead on April 15. On February 22, Clark had relieved Lucas of command, replacing him with Lieutenant General Lucien K. Truscott Jr., but the Allies would not finally fight their way out of Anzio until May 25. Upon realizing the opportunity that had been lost, Winston Churchill remarked disgustedly, "I had hoped we were hurling a wildcat on the shore, but all we got was a beached whale."

Above: A sailor with a US Navy salvage detachment on Anzio tries out what seems to be a locally appropriated Martini-Henry rifle near his bunker living quarters at Anzio on April 15. After March 1944, the Allied beachhead was contained and intermittently under fire from two 215mm Krupp K5 railroad guns that the Germans named "Robert" and "Leopold," and the Americans collectively called "Anzio Annie." After the final Allied breakout, both guns were withdrawn to Civitavecchia and spiked with explosives. The 168th Regiment of the US 34th Infantry Division found them on June 7, and Leopold, the least damaged of the two, now resides at the US Army Ordnance Museum at Aberdeen Proving Grounds, Maryland.

Above: Army troops cover a flamethrower team in eliminating a Japanese position on Bougainville. As it consolidated its gains, the Americal Division was joined by the 93rd Infantry Division, the first black American division committed to combat. By the time the Americans were through, they had killed 8,200 Japanese and another 16,600 of the enemy had succumbed to disease or malnutrition. The Allies began building airfields from which to strike at Rabaul and other Japanese strongholds, while many of the surviving Japanese, cut off to the north and south, established farms to grow their own food.

Right: A Chief Petty Officer mans the control station aboard a US Navy submarine. By the end of 1943, problems with the magnetic exploders on American torpedoes had been remedied and submarines were taking a serious toll on Japanese shipping. Then, on April 13, 1944, Rear Admiral Charles A. Lockwood ordered his captains to target their traditional nemeses, destroyers. By the end of the war, American subs accounted for 39, including four destroyers and two frigates by *Harder* until it was finally sunk off Luzon on August 24 by escort CD-22, and Patrol Boat 102 (ironically, formerly the destroyer USS *Stewart*, captured in Java and reconfigured for Japanese service). *Harder*'s Commander Samuel D. Dealey was posthumously awarded the Medal of Honor.

Below: Corporal H. Langham, at the field phone, and Major Francis O'Brien, members of an RAF Army Air Support Control unit attached to the US Fifth Army in Italy, get a relayed message from a jeep-rigged radio station. They will in turn pass the message on to operators in communication with airmen flying in support of the front-line troops. Ideally, the Army Air Support Control kept in communication with three aircraft at a time—one attacking an enemy target, one en route to take its place, and one refueling and rearming to fly the next sortie.

Above: On April 17, the Japanese army in China launched a massive offensive to secure a swath of territory from Beijing to Indochina, and to push inland the airbases from which Major General Claire Chennault's Fourteenth Air Force had been harassing the Japanese since its formation on March 5, 1943. Dubbed Operation *Ichi-Go* (Number One), the three-phased drive began with 510,000 troops securing the Pinghan Railway between Beijing and Wuhan, followed by the taking of Luoyang on May 25, and the battles of Changsha, Hengyang, Guilin and Lieuzhou. Although *Ichi-Go* achieved its objectives when it concluded on December 10, it left Chennault's air arm still intact and active, while Boeing B-29s of XX Bomber Command, which had been bombing Japan from Chengtu, moved to the Marianas.

Above: The wreckage of an M4 Sherman medium tank and a Bailey Bridge litter the landscape before Monte Cassino in May 1944. On the night of May 17, facing the prospect of being flanked and cut off by Allied progress into the Liri Valley, the last 200 German defenders evacuated Monte Cassino and the next day the 12th Podolian Uhlans of Lieutenant General Wladislaw Ander's Polish II Corps flew their regimental colors from the summit. By May 23, the Allies were breaking through the Gustav and Hitler lines.

Left: Medics of the 100th Infantry Battalion (Separate) evacuate a casualty by jeep. As the Allied forces broke out from Monte Cassino and the Liri Valley, at Anzio General Truscott sent out three American and two British out of his seven available divisions in a two-pronged attack on May 23. Among the units involved was the 100th Battalion, made up of Japanese-American and some Korean residents of Hawaii who had not been deported to detention camps on the mainland. Entering combat with the 34th Infantry Division at Salerno on September 23, 1943, the unit fought with distinction at Cassino and Anzio.

The Hard Road Back I 113

Right: General Clark attaches streamers to the banners of the 100th Infantry Battalion representing its receipt of a Distinguished Unit Citation for exceptional performance of duty at Belvedere and Sassetta on June 26 and 27. On August 2, the 100th Battalion was incorporated into the 442nd Regimental Combat Team, a unit made up of Japanese-American Nisei volunteers from the West Coast, alongside which the 100th had fought throughout the Cassino and Anzio campaigns.

Left: The statue of a Roman official seems to be double-checking the paperwork as Lieutenant Rex Metcalfe pays his soldiers in Rome. On June 2, with the Caesar Line cracking and the German Fourteenth Army engaged in a fighting retreat through the Italian capital, Hitler, fearing another Stalingrad, ordered Field Marshal Kesselring that there should be "no defense of Rome." On the morning of June 5, Fifth Army troops entered an open city.

Right: American soldiers march past the Piazza Venezia and the monument to King Victor Emmanuel II on July 4, during a flag-lowering ceremony following the arrival of General Mark Clark and Secretary of War Henry L. Stimpson in Rome. With the city secured by his troops on June 5, Clark stationed military police around its outskirts to keep British Eighth Army soldiers out—thereby keeping the liberation of Rome a strictly American affair. The very day after Rome's fall to the Allies, however, landings took place in Normandy that would sweep the entire Italian campaign from the headlines.

Chapter 7

The Great Crusade

The Allied seizure of Rome on June 5 was just the start of the single most calamitous month for the Axis. On June 6, Allied forces landed in Normandy, establishing a foothold in France, while in Burma the British 77th Chindit Brigade assaulted Mogaung, securing it on the June 27. On June 15, US Marines landed on Saipan and in history's greatest carrier duel, the Battle of the Philippine Sea on June 19–20, the US Navy tore the heart out of Japan's carrier air arm. On June 22, the Red Army launched Operation Bagration, which by July 4 had retaken Minsk and all but annihilated German Army Group Center, which suffered 300,000 casualties. Only Finland could claim a victory in the Battle of Tali-Ihantala, in which, at terrible cost, it stopped a Soviet offensive between June 25 and July 9 and convinced Josef Stalin to seek separate peace terms from Helsinki.

The rest of the year saw an often costly but nonetheless inexorable Allied advance on all fronts, despite the occasional setback. Romania went over to the Allied side on August 23. Paris was liberated on August 25. Finland agreed to a conditional capitulation and ceasefire on September 5. On September 9, Bulgarians overthrew their royal government and went over to the Allied side. American landings in the Philippines, on October 20, precipitated history's largest naval engagement, the Battle of Leyte Gulf, which left Japan's once-mighty navy in ruins. On November 24, Boeing B-29s left their newly established airbases in the Marianas to bomb Tokyo for the first time.

The end of 1944 saw the Germans launch a counteroffensive against the Americans in the Ardennes, on December 16, and Soviet and Romanian forces encircled Budapest on December 26. The stage was set for the last desperate acts of World War II.

Right: Officers of the Supreme Headquarters of the Allied Expeditionary Force (SHAEF) gather to plan the invasion of German-occupied France in the spring of 1944. Seated, from left, are Air Marshal Sir Arthur Tedder, Deputy Supreme Commander; General Dwight D. Eisenhower, Supreme Commander; and General Bernard L. Montgomery, Commander-in-Chief of British forces. Standing, from left, are Lieutenant General Omar N. Bradley, Senior Commander of US ground forces; Admiral Sir Bertram H. Ramsey, Allied Naval Commander; Air Chief Marshal Sir Trafford Leigh-Mallory, Air Commander-in-Chief; and Lieutenant General Walter Bedell Smith, Chief of Staff.

Below: A US infantry regiment marches through the streets of a British port on its way to the docks, where the troops will be loaded onto landing craft for transport across the English Channel to Normandy. Farther to the northeast, Lieutenant General George Patton was in nominal charge of Operation Fortitude, an invasion force massing for a landing at Calais—involving a nonexistent army backed by inflatable tanks and artillery and dummy aircraft, all to divert German attention from the real target.

Above: An American paratrooper practices with a Thompson submachine gun during maneuvers. Because of their vulnerability to enemy fire while floating down in the chutes, paratroopers were trained to fight and seize the initiative from the instant their boots touched the ground and they regained control of their fate. Such training paid off on D-Day, when bad weather and antiaircraft fire caused the 101st—the first to jump, at 00:48–01:40 hours—and directly following 82nd Airborne troopers to be scattered all over the countryside. Forming small units with whichever comrades they encountered, they wrought chaos in the German rear area.

Above: A barrage balloon, used since the beginning of the war to ensnare low-flying enemy airplanes in the cables hanging underneath, floats above a British port while American troops board the barges that will take them to a troopship for their cross-Channel journey. The first waves of American troops to land were to be the 4th Infantry Division on Utah Beach and the 1st and 29th Infantry divisions on Omaha Beach to its east.

Right: A propaganda picture of a formidable-looking coastal gun as part of Germany's channel defenses embodies the image of Fortress Europe that Adolf Hitler wished to project to his enemies in the West. When assigned to command Army Group B in France, Field Marshal Erwin Rommel was appalled to find how incomplete and neglected the defenses in Normandy actually were, and he took immediate steps to remedy the situation with an increase of beach obstacles and mines.

Right: Canadians come ashore at Juno, lying between British Gold and Sword beaches. At Juno the Canadian Third Division faced elements of the German 716th Division backed by two 155mm and nine 75mm batteries, as well as a sea wall twice the height of that the Americans faced at Omaha Beach. The first wave suffered 50 percent casualties, but enough of their armor got ashore to help secure the beachhead within hours.

Above: A 101st Airborne Division paratrooper poses with a bazooka at the door of a Douglas C-47. While glider-borne troops of the British 6th Airborne Division seized the bascule bridge over the Caen Canal between Caen and Ouistreham, which they named Pegasus Bridge after their shoulder insignia, 45 percent of the 13,000 American paratroops who dropped out of 800 aircraft were scattered around the countryside. In 24 hours, only 2,500 men from the 101st and 2,000 from the 82nd were under division control. Nevertheless, the 82nd Airborne Division claimed to have liberated the first town in France, Sainte-Mère-Église.

Left: Members of the Second Ranger Battalion smile confidently from their landing barge before departing for their objective: six French-made 155mm gun emplacements atop Pointe-du-Hoc, between Utah and Omaha beaches. Using rocket-propelled rope ladders and grapnels, 225 Rangers and Ranger-trained elements of the 116th Infantry Regiment fought their way up the cliffs—only to discover the emplacements empty. The Rangers subsequently found the guns nearby and destroyed them with thermite grenades. Fighting off counterattacks by the 916th Grenadier Regiment and suffering a total of 135 casualties, the Rangers held Pointe-du-Hoc until relieved by the 116th Infantry on June 7.

Above: Canadians man a towed triple Polsten 20mm anti-aircraft battery newly established on Juno Beach. By the end of June 6, 30,000 Canadians had come ashore at Juno and they had advanced 6 miles (10km) into France, the farthest of any of the Allies. That achievement had cost them 1,000 casualties, including 335 dead, and over the next two days the Third Division had to fight off determined counterattacks by the German 21st Panzer and 12th SS "*Hitlerjugend*" Panzer divisions.

Below: Assault engineers practice with a Bangalore torpedo to blow through barbed wire, as used on Omaha Beach, where Colonel George A. Taylor of the 16th Regimental Combat Team (RCT) exhorted his men: "Two kinds of people are staying on this beach, those who are dead and those who are going to die. Now let's get the hell out of here." The 29th Division's Brigadier General Norman Cota similarly rallied the pinned-down 116th RCT. By the end of June 6, both divisions managed to break through and establish a beachhead on Omaha, at a cost of 5,000 casualties.

Below: Supply sergeants check and record blood being shipped in dry ice containers to field hospitals in Normandy on June 12. The British landed successfully at Gold and Sword beaches, but German armor stopped them short of Caen, where they faced weeks of bitter fighting. The American Fourth Infantry Division landed 2,000 yards (1,830m) south of its intended landing place on Utah Beach, but Brigadier General Theodore Roosevelt Jr. improvised an advance from there—thus avoiding the main German defenses. Hitler's Fortress Europe had been breached.

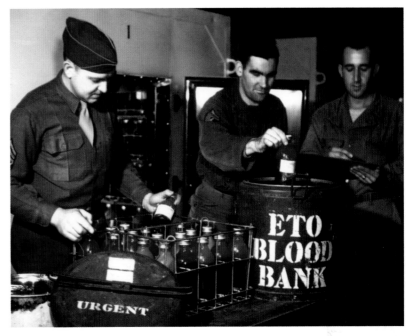

Opposite page: Having loaded their equipment aboard an LCT (landing craft, tank), soldiers of the veteran 1st Infantry Division await the signal for departure. The division's first wave on Omaha Beach, the 16th RCT, drifted east and landed in the face of Normandy's best-prepared defenses, including sea walls up to 12 feet (3.6m) high and members of the German 325th Infantry Division firing from bluffs towering 100–170 feet (30–51m) above them. Only two of the dozen tanks slated to support Omaha made it to the beach. As casualties mounted, General Bradley considered evacuation.

Left: French civilians return to their homes in liberated Cherbourg, a port desperately needed by the Allies to sustain their advance down the Cotentin Peninsula. On June 19, the 4th, 9th, and 79th Infantry Divisions drove north and on June 22 began a general assault. On June 26, the 79th Division captured Fort du Roule, along with Generalleutnant Karl-Wilhelm von Schlieben. Rear Admiral Walter Hennecke wrecked or mined the harbor before he and the last Germans surrendered on June 30, for which Hitler awarded him the Knight's Cross the next day. Engineers soon restored Cherbourg's port facilities to working order.

Opposite page: A truck convoy passes through St. Lô as the American advance resumes. With seven panzer divisions committed against the British and Canadians to the northeast, General Bradley, on July 25, launched Operation Cobra, a breakout from St. Lô that began with an aerial bombardment—some of which accidentally fell on American troops, among whose dead was Lieutenant General Leslie J. McNair. By July 31, the Americans had taken Coutances and Avranches, allowing the First Army to move into Brittany and gaining access to open country for the newly arriving Third Army, under a commander who knew how to use it: Patton.

Above: Waffen SS soldiers man a 75mm antitank gun in the bocage country of the Cotentin Peninsula. Norman farms marked by thick hedge and earthen walls gave the Germans the means to contest the US Army's advance for six weeks following D-Day, ambushing troops and tanks. Meanwhile, German and British tanks—the former including fearsome Tigers and Panthers, the latter including Sherman Fireflies armed with 17-pounders capable of penetrating thick German armor—engaged in a murderous seesaw struggle for Caen.

Above: From left, Lieutenant General Guy G. Symonds, Commander of the II Canadian Corps, Prime Minister Churchill, General Bernard Montgomery, Commander of the 21st Army Group, and Lieutenant General Sir Miles Dempsey, Commander of the British Second Army, review the situation on July 22. On July 18, Montgomery launched Operation Goodwood, an advance to the east of Caen that, after the largest British tank battle thus far in the war, finally drove the Germans out of the city.

Below: Civil Defence crews help rescue injured and dead Londoners from buildings damaged by a V-1 in July 1944. The first *Vergeltungswaffe* ("vengeance weapon"), the V-1 was a gyro-guided, pulse-jet engine-powered flying bomb, the first ten of which were launched on June 13. Among the fighters the RAF mobilized to intercept V-1s was its first jet, the Gloster Meteor. On September 6, the Germans launched the first of 1,115 V-2 rockets, which traveled at twice the speed of sound. By the time attacks ceased in March 1945, 9,551 V-1s had been launched, 2,515 at London, killing 6,184 people and injuring another 17,981.

Right: Battleship *New Mexico*, with *Pennsylvania* lying astern, supports US Marines landing on Saipan on June 15, 1944. While D-Day had involved some 150,000 Allied troops, nearly 130,000 Americans were involved in the Marianas, where the airfields on Saipan, Tinian, and Guam would put new Boeing B-29 Superfortress bombers within striking range of the Japanese Home Islands. The struggle for Saipan climaxed with the largest banzai charge of the war—2,500 on July 3—followed by the mass suicide of almost 1,000 civilians off the cliffs at Marpi Point before the island was declared secure on July 9.

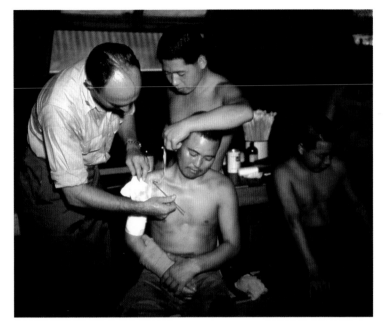

Left: One of 485 prisoners taken on Guam receives medical attention from a US Navy doctor, aided by other POWs. When the Americans landed on July 21, 18,040 Japanese—including Lieutenant General Takeshi Takashina, killed in action on July 28—preferred death to surrender, killing 1,747 Americans and wounding 6,053 before the taking of Mount Barrigada, on August 4, ended organized resistance. Guam was declared secure on August 8, and on August 11 the acting Japanese commander, Major General Hideyoshi Obata, committed suicide. On January 24, 1972, hunters found Sergeant Shoichi Yokoi, a last holdout who had lived in a cave for 27 years.

Opposite page: Crewmen aboard the destroyer *Halford* man 20mm and 40mm guns in anticipation of an air attack off Saipan. On June 19, a Japanese naval force including 9 carriers engaged the Americans' 16 in the Battle of the Philippine Sea, only to lose some 350 planes in an aerial slaughter the F6F pilots called the "Great Mariana Turkey Shoot." Also lost that day were the Japanese flagship carrier *Taiho*, to submarine *Albacore*, and carrier *Shokaku* to submarine *Cavalla*, and on June 20 light carrier *Hiyo* was sunk by Eastern Aircraft TBM-1s from the light carrier *Belleau Wood*.

Above: A German *Sturmgeschütz* (assault gun) III, upgraded with a 75mm antitank gun to offset Germany's shortfall in armor, scouts the steppes as the Red Army advances. Although the Germans continued to take a heavy toll on Soviet armor, they were being overwhelmed and, in the case of Operation Bagration,

even out-generaled as Army Group Center's Third Panzer, Fourth, and Ninth armies were annihilated between June 22 and July 3, 1944, in the worst German defeat of the war. By the end of August, their casualties totaled 550,000 men, 150,000 of whom were prisoners, along with 2,000 tanks and 57,000 other vehicles.

Left: An M-4 Sherman crew of the 752nd Tank Battalion guards a vital crossroads on the road to Pisa. The Allies continued their northward drive up the Italian boot after the fall of Rome, in the face of constant resistance from a succession of defensive lines established in the mountains by Field Marshal Kesselring. On July 20, the Second and Third Battalions of the 442nd Regimental Combat Team fought their way into Pisa, and on July 23 troops of the 34th Infantry Division completed the city's occupation.

Above: An Italian partisan who had taken the Fortress di Basso and engaged German snipers outside Florence, surveys the damaged city on August 14. As the Eighth Army closed in on Florence on August 4, its troops were ordered to avoid fighting there. Declaring it an open city, the Germans evacuated it on August 11, but not before blowing up every bridge across the Arno River save for the medieval Ponte Vecchio, and publicly executing every anti-Nazi partisan and political prisoner in their hands. The British occupied Florence on August 13.

Opposite page: Lance Corporal Sarawan Singh, a military policeman in the Eighth Indian Division, mans a traffic post in Borgo, Italy. The division distinguished itself throughout the campaign, especially during the bloody struggle to break through Kesselring's Green Line—called the "Gothic Line" by the Allies—from August 25 through December 17, 1944. The division's four Victoria Cross recipients included the youngest, 19-year-old Sepoy Kamal Ram of the Third Battalion, Eighth Punjab Regiment, for his single-handed capture of two German machine gun posts and for aiding in eliminating a third along the Garigliano River on May 12, 1944.

Above: Members of a Canadian Highland regiment examine the 20mm guns and rocket launchers on a Hawker Typhoon Mark IB of No. 245 "Northern Rhodesia" Squadron. On orders from Hitler—wounded and shaken after a failed assassination attempt on July 20—the German Seventh and Fifteenth armies unsuccessfully assaulted Mortain and Avranches on August 7. On August 8, Patton's Third Army took Le Mans. Between August 12 and 21, the overextended Germans raced eastward while Allied pincers closed around them at Falaise and Chambois, and Typhoons and other fighter-bombers strafed them on the roads. The Battle of Falaise ended with 50,000 Germans killed or captured.

Right: A 57mm gun crew in St. Malo prepares to shell a nearby island where 700 Germans are holding out. Elements of the 8th and 83rd Infantry Divisions assaulted St. Malo on August 3, but German Colonel Andreas von Aulock put up a determined defense, during which 80 percent of the town was burned. On August 17, P-38J pilot Lieutenant Colonel Seth McKee of the 370th Fighter Group dropped a 165-gallon (624L) fuel tank full of napalm that by pure chance fell through the ventilator shaft of the citadel. Moments later, a white flag went up and the battle of St. Malo was over.

Below: French Foreign Legionnaires train for the coming landing on a North African beach. At 01:30 hours on August 15, 800 members of the 1ère *Commando de l'Afrique du Nord* disembarked from the Canadian command ship *Prince David*, landed at Cap Negre, scaled its 350-foot (106m) cliffs and silenced the guns emplaced at its summit. They then moved inland to secure the road between Toulon and the Riviera, killing 300 Germans and capturing 700, for the loss of 11 commandos killed and 50 wounded.

Left: Captured German army and *Luftwaffe* officers glumly gather for processing aboard a US Navy transport off the coast of southern France following the successful landings on August 15. Judging their position untenable, due as much to spreading French Resistance activity as to the armies they faced, General Johannes Blaskowitz, commanding Army Group G, and General Friedrich Wiese, commanding the 19th Army, offered little more than token resistance before withdrawing from southern France.

Below: LCT-559, LCT-198, and other LCTs and LCMs deliver supplies right to the beach west of St. Raphael on D Plus 5, on August 20. The steel matted ramp in the foreground was laid to help DUKWs drive ashore. Arguably the most important consequence of Operation Dragoon for the overall Allied effort was the liberation of Marseille, along with the Toulon naval base, on August 28. With the logistic line from the Atlantic coast straining to keep up with the Allied advance, Marseilles would provide a third of the materiel necessary to sustain the Allied armies.

Above: Parisians line the Champs Elysées as Allied tanks and half tracks pass through the Arc de Triomphe on August 25, 1944. Although Eisenhower wanted to bypass the French capital, when French Resistance forces there rose up on August 23 General de Gaulle convinced him to dispatch Major General Philippe Leclerc de Hauteclocque's French Second Armored Division and the US Fourth Infantry Division, to liberate the city. Leclerc's advance forces entered Paris on August 24. The next day, German General Dietrich von Choltitz, disobeying Hitler's orders to destroy the city, surrendered to the French.

Right: In a photograph taken by Frank Scherschel, working for *Time* and *Life* magazines, General Charles de Gaulle leads a parade in celebration of the previous day's liberation of Paris on August 26. In September he became president of the Provisional Government of the French Republic, restoring the continuity of the Third Republic and avoiding his country's coming under the authority of an Allied Military Government for Occupied Territories.

Right: Lieutenant Colonel Francis S. Gabreski of the 61st Squadron, 56th Fighter Group, poses in his Republic P-47D Thunderbolt soon after scoring his 28th victory on July 5, 1944, making him the leading American ace in the European Theater of Operations. On July 20, while strafing Bassinheim airfield at what proved to be too low an altitude, "Gabby" Gabreski's propeller bit into the ground and he bellied in, to be taken prisoner. During the Korean War, Colonel Gabreski added six more to his score flying North American F-86E Sabre jets. He died in Long Island, New York, on January 31, 2002.

Above: Crew members of *I'll Get By*, B-17G serial number 42-102700 of the 412th Squadron, 95th Bomb Group, drive up for their next mission from Horham in July 1944. On August 2, *I'll Get By* was shot down and all but three of its ten-man crew—including Oscar Cyrus Walrod, fifth from left—was killed. The 95th was the only group in the Eighth Air Force to receive three Distinguished Unit Citations: for the Regensburg strike on August 17, 1943, Munster on October 10, 1943, and first over Berlin on March 4, 1944.

Right: A British paratrooper undergoes training. On September 18, 1944, British 1st and American 82nd and 101st Airborne Divisions embarked on their largest mission since the war began—Operation Market Garden, an ambitious thrust into the Netherlands to seize a series of bridges and hold them for the following ground forces, culminating with Arnhem's bridge over the Lower Rhine River. A major flaw in the plan was that the Allied advance followed a single road, which, once determined by the Germans, they would do everything to block.

Below: American paratroopers practice on a 75mm pack howitzer, the only artillery that could be airdropped to them. The 101st Airborne Division's role in Market Garden was to seize bridges at Eindhoven, Son, and Veghel, while the 82nd was to take the bridges at Grave and Nijmegan. Despite heavy resistance and the Germans' destruction of the bridge at Son, delaying the Allied advance ten hours while a Bailey bridge was constructed in its place, the Americans achieved their objectives.

Left: Major General Roy Urquhart confers with his staff in February 1945. Dropping into Arnhem on September 18, Urquhart and the First Airborne Division got a nasty surprise to discover the Ninth and Tenth SS Panzer divisions refitting there after the fighting in France. Under overwhelming attacks, the paras were driven from Arnhem on September 21, even as Polish reinforcements of the first independent Parachute Brigade were airdropping into Driel. With ground support still not forthcoming, on September 25 Urquehart evacuated his 2,398 survivors, leaving behind 1,485 dead and 6,414 prisoners, a third of whom were wounded.

Above: General Douglas MacArthur, accompanied by Lieutenant General George C. Kenney, Commander of the Far Eastern Air Force, Lieutenant General Richard K. Sutherland, Chief of Staff, and Major General Verne D. Mudge, Commander of the First Cavalry Division, inspect the beachhead on Leyte, after the landings that marked his long-promised return to the Philippines on October 20. The men who stormed ashore came from Lieutenant General Walter Krueger's Sixth Army, supported by both Vice Admiral Thomas C. Kinkaid's Seventh and Admiral William F. Halsey's Third Fleets.

Above: From left, Admiral William Halsey poses for the camera with Secretary of the Navy Frank Knox and Chief of Naval Operations Ernest D. King, after Halsey received a gold staff in lieu of a second Distinguished Service Medal in January 1944. On October 25, Halsey led his entire Third Fleet to Cape Engaño to sink four Japanese carriers that had few planes and were intended all along as decoys; the aim was to draw him away from the beachhead at Leyte while the main Japanese battle fleet slipped in to destroy it.

Above: A Curtiss SB2C-4 dive bomber revs up its engine aboard a *Casablanca* class escort carrier. Faced with Vice Admiral Takeo Kurita's battle force off Samar Island on October 25, Rear Admiral Clifton Sprague's Task Unit 77.1.3 carried out a heroic fighting retreat that cost it the escort carrier *Gambier Bay*, destroyers *Johnston* and *Hoel*, and destroyer escort *Samuel B. Roberts*. In the process, it sank heavy cruisers *Suzuya*, *Chokai*, and *Chikuma*, and miraculously caused Kurita, who thought he was facing fleet carriers, to withdraw, saving the beachhead. Soon afterward, escort carrier St. Lô was sunk in the war's first kamikaze attack.

Left: On December 15, 1944, P-38 L pilot Major Richard Ira Bong shot down a Nakajima Ki.43 fighter bomber trying to attack American shipping off Mindoro in the Philippines. On December 17, he was credited with another, raising his score to 40 and his status to American Ace of Aces. At that point Bong, who had received the Medal of Honor, went home, married his hometown sweetheart, Marjorie Vattendahl, and became a test pilot, only to be killed while test flying a Lockheed P-80 jet fighter on August 6, 1945.

Left: Concrete "Dragon's Teeth," emplaced to impede Allied tanks, were just one obstacle in the "Siegfried Line," as the Allies nicknamed Germany's border defenses. Entering Lorraine on September 5, Patton's Third Army became mired in a costly, slow battle of attrition against the region's fortresses, culminating in the fall of Metz on November 23. To the north, the First Army entered the Hürtgen Forest on September 19 and was soon stopped in its tracks. It took the First Army from October 2 to 21 to take Aachen, the first city on German soil to surrender to Allied invaders.

Left: An American tank destroyer pauses beside a second tank that has slid off the road during the Battle of the Bulge. On December 16, 600,000 Germans in 29 divisions attacked through the Ardennes Forest in a bid to smash through American forces and retake the Belgian port of Antwerp. Although they inflicted heavy casualties, however, they never got close to their goal and failed to capture the crossroads town of Bastogne before Patton's Third Army swung north to relieve its beleaguered defenders led by the 101st Airborne Division's Brigadier General Anthony McAuliffe.

Above: Privates First Class Percy E. Laney and William Peebles of the all-black 92nd Infantry Division's signal company troubleshoot telephone lines near Villareggio, Italy. During a German counterattack at Sommocolonia on December 26, First Lieutenant John R. Fox, a forward observer of the division's 598th Field Artillery Battalion attached to the 366th Infantry, called artillery down on the attackers and ultimately on his own position. When the Americans retook the town the next day, they found Fox's body, surrounded by those of 100 dead Germans. On January 13, 1997, Fox was posthumously awarded the Medal of Honor.

Chapter 8

Nemesis

Although the New Year opened with a German offensive into Alsace, a surge of *Luftwaffe* fighter activity meant to cripple tactical Allied airbases throughout France and Belgium, and a series of thrusts into Hungary. However, all of those efforts failed, only hastening the Reich's inevitable downfall. Adolf Hitler, descending deeper into madness since the failed assassination attempt of July 20, 1944, adopted a mindset that, if the German people could not conquer the world, then they must all die with him in a fiery Wagnerian *Götterdämmerung*. Motivated as much by fear of the Russians as by fear of SS execution, the Germans fought on.

Japan, too, clung to a policy of fighting to the death. This took the form of well-planned stubborn defenses designed to inflict the maximum casualties on the Allies, as at Iwo Jima and Okinawa, and the use of suicide weapons, guided to their targets by airmen and seamen who were ordered to destroy the enemy's ships and planes at the price of their own lives.

The result of both attitudes was that 1945 would see some of the bloodiest fighting of the war before the Allied pincers closed on the Reich at last in April. Benito Mussolini died ignominiously at the hands of his own people on April 28. Hitler committed suicide within his bunker on the April 30, as Soviet forces overran Berlin. Japan's militarists mobilized the country for an Allied invasion, but the dropping of two atomic bombs on the cities of Hiroshima and Nagasaki, combined with the devastating entry of Soviet forces into Manchuria, finally convinced all but the most fanatical that the situation for Japan was hopeless. On August 14, Emperor Hirohito announced his acceptance of unconditional surrender. On the deck of the battleship *Missouri*, World War II formally ended, six years and one day after it had begun.

Left: German infantry take up a holding position as their forces withdraw along the Northern Front. Driven from Finland, the Germans resisted the Red Army's advance through East Prussia in fortresses such as Courland and Küstrin. To the south, attempts to retake Budapest and the Danube River with Operations Konrad I (January 1, 1945), II (January 7) and III (January 17), failed. Budapest fell on February 13, and Breslau followed the next day. On March 6, the war's last German offensive, Operation Spring Awakening, drove toward Lake Balaton but was stopped on March 14, and two days later the Soviets counterattacked.

Right: M-4 Shermans of the 40th Tank Battalion, Seventh Armored Division, line up outside St. Vith, Belgium. The Seventh Armored Division had fought alongside the 106th Infantry Division at St. Vith, in the face of the German Ardennes offensive between December 17 and 22. The Americans were forced to abandon the town, although had managed to set back the Germans' time schedule by five days. On January 20, the Seventh Armored Division returned to participate in the counterattack to retake the town.

Above: A mortar team deals with German resistance outside of St. Vith on January 24, as the general Allied counterattack continues. By January 31, the German army had been driven back to the positions it had occupied before the Ardennes offensive began. Operations *Bodenplatte* (Base Plate), a massed fighter bomber attack on Allied airbases, and *Nordwind* (North Wind), an attack on the Seventh Army in Alsace, both launched on January 1, also failed to achieve their objectives, serving only to leave both the *Luftwaffe* and the German army further depleted.

Left: Winston Churchill, Franklin D. Roosevelt, and Josef Stalin are photographed in the courtyard of Livadia Palace during a recess in the Big Three Conference at Yalta, in the Soviet Crimea, which began on February 4, 1945. The three heads of state determined, among other issues, the division of Germany as well as the extent of their respective spheres of influence after the war. The latter agreement would result in Poland, Hungary, and Czechoslovakia falling under Soviet domination for the next 45 years.

Right: A 37mm gun crew of Company I, 189th Regiment, 37th Infantry Division, fires at Japanese defending the west wall of Manila's Intramuros in late February. On January 9, the US Sixth Army landed in Lingayen Gulf, Luzon, joined on January 31 by the Eighth Army, which landed at Nasugbu. On February 3, the Americans liberated Santo Tomás University, which had been converted to a prison camp. The next day, they entered Manila, which was fanatically defended by Rear Admiral Sanji Iwabuchi and 14,000 naval and army personnel. When the city was finally secured on March 3, 1,010 Americans and 12,000 Japanese were dead, along with about 100,000 Filipino civilians.

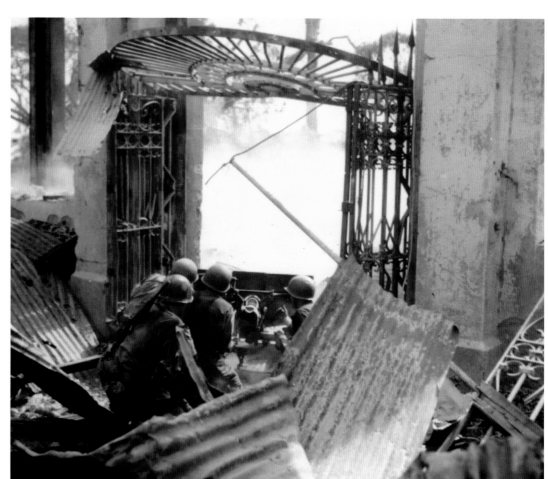

Above: Medics of the Tenth Mountain Division tend to casualties. The specially trained division entered combat on January 28, 1945, when it assaulted the much-contested ridge between Monte Belvedere and Monte della Torraccia in the northern Appenines. On February 19, the 85th and 87th Regiments staged a surprise bayonet rush without artillery support to take Monte Belvedere, and they held it against seven German counterattacks in two days. The fighting cost the division 195 dead and 655 wounded, but they took 1,000 prisoners and opened the way into the Po Valley.

Above: Wrecked vehicles and casualties litter the beach on Iwo Jima on February 19, 1945, as the marines fight their way to the airfield and toward Mount Suribachi, from which Japanese artillery was turning the embattled beachhead into a charnel house. The marines called Iwo "hell," to which Navy photographer Paul Guttman, who spent several days there, added, "It even smelled like hell," recalling the sulfurous fumes that emanated from the volcanic ash.

Opposite page: Amphibious tractors carry marines toward Iwo Jima. Possessing an airfield that could accommodate damaged B-29s unable to return to the Marianas and could serve as a base for fighter escorts of the Seventh Air Force, Iwo was of strategic importance. However, its 22,785 defenders, brilliantly commanded by Lieutenant General Tadamichi Kuribayashi, had prepared an extraordinarily extensive network of defenses throughout the 3-mile (4.8km) island and were under orders to inflict maximum casualties on the Americans.

Above: Mount Suribachi becomes the epicenter of an intense naval and aerial bombardment on February 19, while an LCS(L) (landing craft, support, large) and several smaller craft land reinforcements. On the fifth day of the battle, the marines finally fought their way to the summit of the 545-foot (166m) strongpoint and raised a flag, which was later replaced by a larger one to ensure that the bombardment would cease. Joe Rosenthal's picture of the second flag raising became a Marine Corps icon, but it was only the beginning—fighting would continue across the rest of the island until March 26.

Below: A Gurkha attached to the British Fourteenth Army in Burma poses with a Sten submachine gun and traditional kukri. Near Tamandu on March 5, *Havildar* (sergeant) Bhanbhagta Gurung of Third Battalion, Second (King Edward VII's Own) Gurkha Rifles, exposed himself in order to pick off a Japanese sniper; he then advanced alone to eliminate four Japanese defensive positions with rifle, bayonet, and grenades. He then assaulted a bunker with two smoke grenades and killed the three-man machine gun crew with his kukri. For that action, he became one of 12 Gurkhas to be awarded the Victoria Cross during World War II.

Left: Amid the British Fourteenth Army's campaign to retake central Burma, Indian machine gunners take up position on Mandalay Hill, while Fort Dufferin comes under British attack in the background. On February 28, 1945, British forces entered Meiktila, securing it and its strategically vital airbase on March 1, and subsequently holding the objective against a succession of Japanese counterattacks until March 28. In a parallel effort, on March 8, the 19th Indian Division stormed Mandalay Hill.

Right: Burial services are held aboard the destroyer *Hansford* for a marine who had died of his wounds while en route from Iwo to Saipan. Only 219 of Iwo's defenders surrendered; the rest, including Kuribayashi, died after killing 6,821 Americans and wounding another 19,217. In addition to the marine casualties, the supporting fleet suffered its share on February 21, when six suicide planes badly damaged the carrier *Saratoga*, which lost 123 men killed or missing, and two others sank the escort carrier *Bismarck Sea*, with 318 of its crew.

Left: British soldiers look down from Mandalay's Pagoda Hill to observe their comrades' progress at Fort Dufferin. With his 15th Division seriously understrength after months of fighting, Lieutenant General Seiei Yamamoto was not in favor of holding Mandalay, but his superiors ordered him to defend it to the death. The Japanese duly repulsed several British attempts to storm Fort Dufferin, including advances through the sewers. Finally, after convincing his commanders that further resistance would be futile, Yamamoto and the remains of his division slipped out of the fort through the same sewer system on March 21.

Right: Photographer's Mate Paul D. Guttman took this photograph of a Yokosuka P1Y1 bomber about to crash after being hit by anti-aircraft fire during attacks on Task Force 58 during carrier strikes on the Japanese Home Islands on March 19, 1945. The only Japanese success occurred when a dive bomber slipped in to score two 550-pound (249kg) bomb hits on the carrier *Franklin*, causing fires that killed 724 men, injured 265, and nearly sank the ship.

Above: Trucks of the Seventh Army cross the Alexander Patch
Heavy Pontoon Bridge, built by the 85th Engineer Battalion,
across the Rhine River at Worms, Germany, on March 28. To the
north, the First Army's Ninth Infantry Division discovered a bridge
across the Rhine still intact at Remagen on March 7 and fought
its way across. The Germans counterattacked and struck at the
bridge with V-2 rockets, Me-262A2a fighter bombers, and Arado
Ar-234B jet bombers, but by the time it finally collapsed on
March 17 the 51st and 291st Engineer battalions had built
pontoon and Bailey Bridges to keep the traffic going.

Right: Landing craft, infantry LCI-809, and other landing craft of
various sizes head for the beach on Okinawa on April 1, 1945.
Facing the US Army and Marine troops were the 120,000
Japanese of Lieutenant Mitsuru Ushijima's 32nd Army, which
pursued a policy of fighting retreat into the southern portion
of the island while inflicting as much attrition as possible on
the Americans.

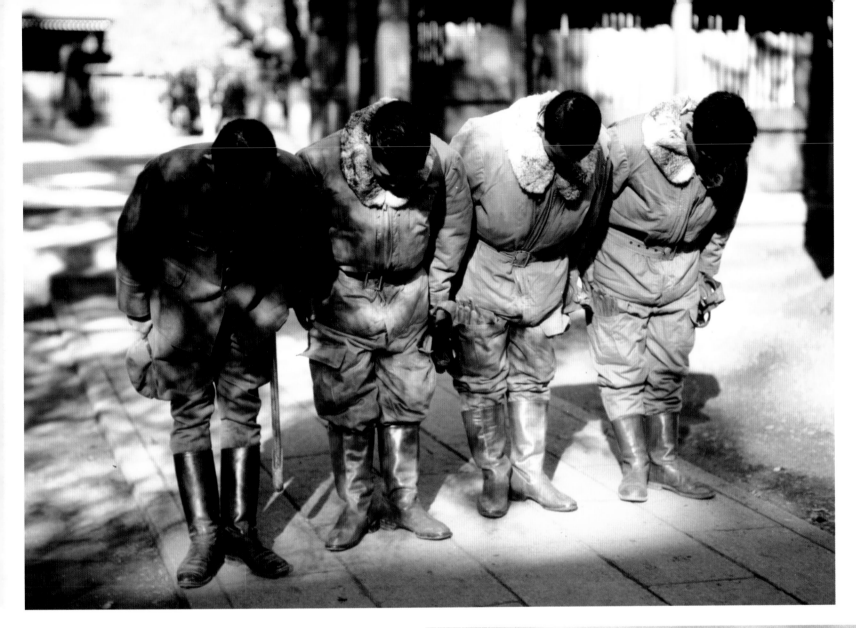

Above: Japanese airmen perform a postwar reenactment of the ceremony preceding a *kamikaze* ("divine wind") mission. Okinawa saw a crescendo of suicide attacks, including *kamikaze* aircraft, explosive-packed one-man *Shinyo* ("ocean shaker") boats, and an attempt by the battleship *Yamato* to run aground off Okinawa and fire all its ammunition at the Americans—only to be sunk en route by carrier planes on April 7. The attacks also included an airplane belly landing on Yontan airfield on the night of May 24–25, disgorging grenade-armed *Giretsu* ("heroic") commandos who destroyed seven planes and two large fuel tanks before being killed off.

Right: Americans guard a Yokosuka MXY7 rocket-powered man-guided bomb captured on Okinawa. Called *Ohka* ("cherry blossom") by the Japanese but codenamed *Baka* ("Idiot") by the Americans, the MXY7 was launched from a specially modified G4M2e bomber. One damaged a 16-inch (400mm) turret on the battleship *West Virginia* on April 1, and another sank the destroyer *Mannert L. Abele* on April 12, but the vast majority went down with their bombers at the hands of American fighters before they even reached the Fifth Fleet.

Left: A Supermarine Seafire Mark IB pilot waits for the order to climb aboard for his next mission from the carrier *Indomitable*. Intended as ship-borne interceptors, Seafires first saw action over Salerno in September 1943, but later-model Seafire Mark IIIs came fully into their own during the Okinawa campaign, defending *Indomitable* and other carriers of Task Force 57 from *kamikazes*. Meanwhile, their longer-range aircraft attacked airfields in the Sakahima Gunto and Ishigaki Shima, from which Formosa-based suicide planes staged before trying to strike at the Fifth Fleet from the south.

Left: Escorted by motor police and armed forces personnel, the casket bearing Franklin D. Roosevelt's body passes up Constitution Avenue toward the White House on April 14. At 15:35 in the afternoon of April 12, 1945, the President died of what his cardiologist, Dr. Howard Bruenn, diagnosed as "a massive brain hemorrhage." Churchill remarked that, upon learning the news, "I was overpowered by a sense of deep and irreparable loss." The Japanese broadcast condolences to the Americans. Hitler celebrated the news as a miracle that would turn the war around in his favor.

Left: A B-29 takes off from Harmon Field, Guam, for another strike against the Japanese Home Islands on April 13. After taking command of the Twentieth Air Force, Major General Curtis E. LeMay eschewed many of the tactics used in the strategic bombing campaign in Europe, reducing the defensive armament on the B-29s and sending them over Japan in high-speed, low-altitude raids using incendiary bombs. Attacking Tokyo on the night of March 10, the bombers burned 250,000 homes and killed 100,000 civilians.

Right: Patrol torpedo boats enter Polloo Harbor in support of the 24th Infantry Division's landing at Parang, Mindanao, on April 17. Scouting and ambushing from the Mediterranean to the Solomons and the Philippines, PT boat crews installed supplements to their torpedoes ranging from the twin .50-caliber guns on the vessel in foreground to 20mm cannons. Begun on March 10, the Eighth Army's brilliantly conducted Mindanao campaign was aided by Filipino guerrillas to limit American deaths to 820, a small number compared to 10,000 Japanese killed in action and another 8,000 of starvation and disease when the remaining 22,000 Japanese surrendered on August 15.

Right: Soldiers of Patton's Third Army learn about life and death in Buchenwald concentration camp from the inmates on April 18, 1945. On April 11, the Ninth Armored Infantry Battalion of the Sixth Armored Division under Captain Frederick Keffner had been first to liberate the camp. On April 25, the British 11th Armoured Division liberated Bergen-Belsen, where 60,000 died, including diarist Anne Frank. On April 29, the Seventh Army liberated the first concentration camp, Dachau, where 32,000 had died.

Below: Third Army troops gather around a truck containing 40 bodies before crematoria at Buchenwald on April 18. An estimated 56,545 of the 238,380 people kept at Buchenwald died or were murdered. Farther east, especially in Poland, the Nazi "Final Solution" was pursued more efficiently. On July 22, 1944, the Red Army liberated the prisoners at Majdanek, where 78,000 people had been put to death. On January 27, 1945, they secured Auschwitz-Birkenau, in time to free 7,500 inmates, but too late for the 780,863 who had been exterminated therein or shot along the road as they were herded west to other death camps.

Below: Members of the 273rd Regiment, 69th Infantry Division, meet allies of the 175th Rifle Regiment, 58th Guards Division, at Torgau on the Elbe River on April 25. In Berlin, Marshal Zhukov's forces were bringing down the curtain on the Third Reich, street by street. On April 30, Adolf Hitler and his newly married mistress, Eva Braun, died in a suicide pact. That night, Mikhail P. Minin raised the Soviet flag above the Reichstag, but it was knocked down during a German counterattack. On May 2, Berlin surrendered and another flag was raised by Alyosha Kovalyov, a scene photographed by Evgeny Khaldei.

Above: German prisoners taken by the VI Corps of the Fifth Army in northern Italy. On April 6, the US Fifth Army and British Eighth Army jointly advanced across the Lombardy Plains, aided by Italian partisans, who helped by tying down or trapping Axis forces until the Germans, learning of Hitler's death, surrendered. Benito Mussolini and his mistress, Clara Petacci, were caught by partisans near Lake Como while trying to flee to Switzerland on April 27. The two were shot at Mezzegra the next day and hung by their heels in an Esso gas station near Milan on April 29.

Left: *Wehrmacht* Chief of Staff *Generaloberst* Alfred Jodl, flanked by Major Wilhelm Oxenius and General Admiral Hans-Georg Friedeberg, Deputy Commander of U-boats, signs articles of unconditional surrender to the Allies at Reims, France, on May 8, 1945. In accordance with Hitler's last orders, Grand Admiral Karl Dönitz took charge of a provisional government in Flensburg as *Reichspräsident*, but on May 23 the Allies dissolved it. On the same day, Friedeberg committed suicide and *Reichsführer* Heinrich Himmler, captured by the British the day before, did likewise with potassium cyanide. On June 5, Germany came under military government by the Allied Occupation Forces.

Left: New Yorkers take to the streets of downtown Manhattan after news arrives of Germany's surrender, near a model of the Statue of Liberty. Similar V-E (Victory in Europe) Day celebrations were taking place all over the Western world, from London to Moscow. In the Far East, however, there remained a job to be done. On April 9, 80,000 Japanese advanced into west Hunan, where they were opposed by 100,000 Chinese army and guerrilla soldiers, backed by their own air arm and Chennault's Fourteenth Air Force. By June 7, the Japanese had been thrown back with an admitted 27,000 casualties.

Below: At Berchtesgaden on June 7, American troops ceremoniously raise the Stars and Stripes over the former headquarters of Field Marshal Wilhelm Keitel, Chief of the German General Staff.

Left: *U-858,* an ocean going Type IXC submarine, arrives at Cape Henlopen, Delaware, in May 1945, after learning of the German surrender and surfacing to capitulate at sea. Lieutenant Commander Willard D. Michael, with megaphone in the conning tower, serves as officer in charge. Above floats a blimp along with a new American innovation, a Sikorski HNS-1 helicopter. By the end of the war the German U-boat arm had lost 30,000 out of the 40,000 personnel who had carried out Dönitz's undersea war.

Above: Spoils of war: A Messerschmitt Me-262A-1a jet fighter is readied for flight testing and shipment to the United States by Colonel Harold E. Watson's 54th Air Disarmament Squadron, also known as "Watson's Whizzers," in June 1945. Although its combat debut in July 1944 was too late to save the Reich, the Me-262, with other captured German technology, advanced the progress of aviation in all of the Allied countries into whose hands it fell.

Above: Another Nazi "wonder weapon" that failed to win the war but changed the future was the V-2 rocket, an American-captured example of which undergoes testing under the US Army's Ordnance peacetime program of scientific research and development at White Sands, New Mexico, on May 10, 1946. From the V-2's technology sprang the nuclear-tipped guided missiles that dominated the Cold War between the West and the Warsaw Pact until 1989, and the American and Soviet space programs that led to humans orbiting the Earth and walking on the moon.

Opposite page: The British passenger liner-turned-troopship *Queen Mary* arrived in New York City on June 20, with thousands of American troops on board. Those with sufficient combat points on their record might receive honorable discharges, but for thousands of others who had not seen enough service prior to Germany's surrender, the next destination would likely be the Pacific for the projected invasion of Japan.

Above: The leading surviving Nazi officials facing trial for war crimes and crimes against humanity before the International Military Tribunal in Nuremburg's Palace of Justice listen intently to the court proceedings. Seated in the front row from left are Hermann Göring, Rudolf Hess, Joachim von Ribbentropp, Wilhelm Keitel and Alfred Rosenberg. In the back row from left are Grand Admirals Karl Dönitz and Erich Reader, former Hitler Youth leader Baldur von Shirach, and Fritz Sauckel and Alfred Jodl.

Left: Major General Leslie R. Groves headed the development of one secret weapon in which the United States was ahead of both Germany and Japan. Harnessing the fruits of research provided by refugee physicists such as Albert Einstein from Germany, Enrico Fermi from Italy, and Hungarians Leo Szilard and Edward Teller, Groves and American physicist J. Robert Oppenheimer pursued the Manhattan Project, toward the conversion of energy from the fission of uranium isotope into a super bomb.

Right: The Japanese port of Hiroshima lies in ruins after becoming the target of the first atomic bomb, "Little Boy," dropped from *Enola Gay*, a B-29 of the Tinian-based 509th Composite Group on August 6, 1945. Amid the meeting of Churchill and Stalin with President Harry Truman at Potsdam, Germany, between July 17 and August 2, Truman issued the Potsdam Declaration on July 26, calling on Japan to unconditionally surrender or face "prompt and utter destruction." Japan's failure to respond led to the first nuclear bombing in history and the death of some 70,000 people.

Above: The first atomic bomb test takes place near Alamogordo, New Mexico, on July 16, 1945. Allegedly the first remark from J. Robert Oppenheimer, who was primarily responsible for the development of the device, was simply, "It works." Later, as the import of what he had seen sank in, he quoted the *Bhagavad Gita*: " I am become death, the destroyer of worlds."

Above: Dr. Nagai, medical instructor and X-ray specialist at Nagasaki Hospital, wanders amid the ruins of his city a month after the atomic bomb "Fat Man" was dropped on it by the B-29 *Bockscar*. On August 9, the Soviet Union declared war on Japan and its forces swept into Manchuria, sweeping the Kwantung Army before them. In response to further silence from Japan regarding surrender, *Bockscar* had been sent to Kokura, but after encountering 70-percent cloud cover it bombed the secondary target, Nagasaki, instead, killing at least 40,000 people.

Above: Japanese representatives sign the surrender documents aboard the battleship Missouri in Tokyo Bay on September 2, 1945. On August 14, Emperor Hirohito, despite a coup attempt the previous day by army officers intent on fighting on, announced his intent to surrender. Although fighting would continue in places, particularly against still-advancing Soviet forces in Manchuria, Korea, and the Kurile Islands, throughout most of the bypassed remnants of its empire Japanese forces were standing down and surrendering prior to the final, formal gathering aboard *Missouri*.

Left: General Douglas MacArthur, with American Lieutenant General Jonathan Wainright and British Lieutenant General Arthur E. Percival standing behind him, signs the surrender papers aboard *Missouri*. Wainright, who had surrendered American forces in the Philippines in April 1942, and Percival, who had done so at Singapore in February, were freed from Hsian Prison, Manchuria, by Office of Strategic Services agents and brought to the ceremony. After bringing the world conflict to an end exactly six years and one day after it began, MacArthur announced, simply, "These proceedings are now closed."

Right: Homecoming British soldiers and local civilians pose aboard a Universal Carrier at Butlin's Holiday Camp at Filey, Yorkshire, in August 1945. Despite the country's achievement, the war left Britain's economy in a shambles and the surrender of Singapore to the Japanese in February 1942 had shattered the image of European supremacy throughout Asia. Over the next 15 years, the British Empire crumbled away, though it was largely replaced by a Commonwealth as many of the newly independent nations sought to maintain friendly trade relations with the former power that had liberated them from the harsher rule of the Japanese.

Below: Wrecked or disabled fighters of the Japanese 302nd *Kokutai* (naval air group) litter Astugi Airport in September 1945. Among the types that fought Japan's last air battles were, from foreground, the Mitsubishi A6M5 Zero (codenamed "Zeke" by the Allies), the Mitsubishi J2M3 *Raiden* ("thunderbolt") interceptor, (codename "Jack") and the Nakajima J1N1-S *Gekko* ("moonlight") night fighter, codenamed "Irving."

Left: The defenses that Japan never brought into play included these 59 Type D *Koryu* ("scaly dragon") 60-ton (54 tonnes) midget submarines lined up in a flooded drydock at Kure, photographed in February 1946. Carrying a five-man crew and two 17.7-inch (450mm) torpedoes at a submerged speed of 16 knots (29kph), 115 of these submarines were completed and another 500 were in various stages of construction when the war ended.

Below: Andrei Gromyko, Soviet ambassador to the United States and an early delegate to the United Nations, addresses the Security Council from the rostrum during the organization's first meeting in Central Hall Westminster, London, on January 17, 1946. Conceived in 1942 to replace the League of Nations, the United Nations Organization was officially founded on October 24, 1945, with permanent members the United States, United Kingdom, Soviet Union, Republic of China, and France, as well as 46 other sovereign nations. The United Nations' headquarters were established in New York between 1949 and 1952.

Above: Hideki Tojo, former Prime Minister, faces seven counts of war crimes at the International Military Tribunal for the Far East in Tokyo. Forced to resign as Prime Minister on July 18, 1944, Tojo was one of 40 key Japanese leaders at whom MacArthur leveled war crimes charges. When arrested at his home in Setagaya, he shot himself four times in the chest but was hospitalized and healed in time to be convicted on November 12, 1948, and hanged on December 23.

Picture Credits

Acknowledgments

Gina McNeely would like to thank Brooke McNeely for technical assistance and Susannah Jayes for additional picture research. Jon Guttman wishes to acknowledge the technical assistance from brother Robert Guttman and colleague Laura Pfost in the course of preparing the text. Elephant Book Company would like to thank Phil Jarrett and Lawrence Paterson.